ROBERT MOSES
SINGLE-MINDED GENIUS

Papers presented at Long Island Studies Conference,
Robert Moses and the Planned Environment,
June 10–11, 1988,
sponsored by Long Island Studies Institute,
Hofstra Cultural Center, Hofstra University,
Hempstead, Long Island, New York.

Cover by Anne R. Knight

LONG ISLAND STUDIES

ROBERT MOSES
SINGLE-MINDED GENIUS

Edited by
Joann P. Krieg

Heart of the Lakes Publishing
Interlaken, New York
1989

Copyright © 1989
Long Island Studies Institute
Hofstra University, Hempstead, NY 11550
All rights reserved

This publication was made possible, in part,
by a New York State Legislative Grant.

Excerpts from *The Power Broker: Robert Moses and the Fall of New York*
by Robert A. Caro. Copyright © 1974 by Robert A. Caro. Reprinted
by permission of Alfred A. Knopf, Inc.

Library of Congress Cataloging-in-Publication Data

Robert Moses: Single-Minded Genius.

(Long Island studies)
Papers presented at the Conference on Long Island Studies: "Robert Moses and the Planned Environment," June 10–11, 1988, sponsored by Long Island Studies Institute, Hofstra University.
Includes index.
1. Moses, Robert, 1888–1981—Congresses. 2. Regional planners—New York (State)—Long Island—Biography—Congresses. 3. Regional planning—New York (State)—Long Island—Congresses. I. Krieg, Joann P. II. Conference on Robert Moses and the Planned Environment (1988 : Hofstra University) III. Series.

HT393.N72L67   1989   974.7'04'0924 [B]   88-34768
ISBN: 1-55787-040-3 (cloth); 1-55787-041-1 (pbk.)

Manufactured in the United States of America

A *quality* publication of
Heart of the Lakes Publishing
Interlaken, New York 14847

Contents

Robert Moses	9
The Legacy of Robert Moses	10
Introduction Joann P. Krieg	13

Re-evaluating the Power Broker

Robert Moses and the Planned Environment:
    A Re-evaluation
    Kenneth T. Jackson
	21

Some Reflections on Moses and his Biographer Jameson W. Doig	31
Robert Caro's Moses: A Historian's Critique George Stevens	35
Robert Caro and His Critics Karen E. Markoe	47

Limiting Power

How to Rein in and Reshape Robert Moses:
    the Port Authority's Varied Strategies
    Jameson W. Doig
	57

The Moses Model of Governance David C. Perry	69

Rockefeller, Moses, and the Bridge
    That Never Was
    Peter Bales
	79

Queens County

From Dump to Glory: Robert Moses and the
Flushing Meadow Improvement
Helen A. Harrison — 91

Robert Moses and the New Deal in Queens
Jeffrey A. Kroessler — 101

The Man Who Changed the Map of Queens:
A Personal View
David Oats — 109

Photographic Essay

Open Spaces ... Public Places — 117

Nassau and Suffolk Counties

The Building of Jones Beach
Robert Moses — 135

Robert Moses: Long Island's First Environmentalist
John A. Black — 141

The Long Island Motor Parkway: Prelude to Robert Moses
Robert Miller — 151

Building the Roads to Greatness: Robert Moses
and Long Island's State Parkways
J. Lance Mallamo — 159

An Inside View of Jones Beach
Peter L. Kramer — 169

Robert Moses as Hofstra Trustee, 1943–1956:
Potent Preeminence to Petty Politics
Natalie A. Naylor — 175

The Moses Design

The Rustic and the Sophisticated in Park Design:
The Moses Style vs. the CCC Design
Frank B. Burggraf and Karen Rollet — 191

Contents

The Best Laid Plans: Robert Moses and
    the Making of Metroland
    Mollie Keller 203

The Public Works of Aymar Embury II in
    New York City and Long Island
    Peter S. Kaufman 213

Contributors 219

Index 223

Courtesy of Hofstra University Archives

Robert Moses

Robert Moses

Robert Moses was born December 18, 1888 in New Haven, Connecticut to Emanuel and Bella (Cohen) Moses. He received his first degree, a B.A., from Yale University in 1909. Two years later Oxford University granted him a B.A. with honors in jurisprudence, and an M.A. in 1911. In 1914 Columbia University awarded him a Ph.D.

He began his public career in 1913, and for decades afterward he headed park, transportation, and power agencies in New York State, as chairman of the State Council of Parks and as president of the Long Island State Park Commission (1924–1963). For thirty years, 1933–1963, Moses was chairman of the Jones Beach State Parkway Authority and of the Bethpage Park Authority. Between 1934 and 1960 he was New York City park commissioner, chairman of the Triborough Bridge Authority, 1936–1946, chairman of the consolidated Triborough Bridge and New York City Tunnel Authority, 1946–1968, and chairman of the New York Power Authority, 1954–1963.

Moses served as New York's Secretary of State, 1927–1937, and was Republican candidate for governor in 1934. He had the distinction of being the sole member of the Henry Hudson Parkway Authority and Marine Parkway Authority from 1934 to 1938, was the Executive Officer of the New York City World's Fair Commission, 1936–1940, and President of the New York World's Fair Corporation, 1960–1967. Between the Fairs he served on the New York City Planning Commission, chairing a slum clearance committee, coordinating arterial projects, and as a member of a city-wide transportation council.

While serving in all these capacities, Moses still found time to be a consultant to numerous governmental agencies and to private industry, give speeches and write books, be a lecturer at colleges and universitites, and serve on the Board of Trustees of Hofstra College. He was a recipient of countless awards and medals, an honorary member of many organizations and an active participant in more of these than would seem possible given the scope of his commitments. In the turbulent decade of the 1960s, Moses was director of Lincoln Center for the Performing Arts.

Near his death, in 1981, he was leading what was for him a quiet life, writing newspaper articles and giving interviews, in most of which he battled old—and new—enemies, that is, those who could not see the wisdom of his productive but somewhat autocratic ways.

The Legacy of Robert Moses

Roadways on Long Island

Interborough Parkway, 1935	Grand Central Parkway, 1936
Cross Island Parkway, 1940	Shore Parkway (Belt), 1941
Van Wyck Expressway, 1950	Prospect Expressway, 1955
Clearview Expressway, 1963	Brooklyn-Queens Expressway, 1964
Gowanus Expressway, 1964	Whitestone Expressway, 1972
Southern State Parkway, 1927	Wantagh State Parkway, 1929
Northern State Parkway, 1930s–1952	Meadowbrook Parkway, 1934
Long Island Expressway, 1940	Sagtikos State Parkway, 1952
Robert Moses Parkway, 1954	Sunken Meadow Parkway, 1957
Seaford-Oyster Bay Expressway, 1969	Long Island Expressway to Riverhead, 1972

Other Roadways

West Side Highway, 1937	Henry Hudson Parkway, 1938
Hutchinson River Parkway, 1941	Bronx River Parkway, 1951
F. D. R. Drive, 1954	New England Thruway, 1958
Major Deegan Expressway, 1961	Bruckner Expressway, 1961
Harlem River Drive, 1962	Cross Bronx Expressway, 1963

Robert Moses Parkway, Niagara River, 1964

Buildings

United Nations, 1952	New York Coliseum, 1956
Lincoln Center, 1962	Shea Stadium, 1964
World's Fair, 1964	

Bridges and Tunnels

Henry Hudson, 1936	Triborough, 1936
Marine Parkway, 1937	Cross Bay, 1939
Whitestone, 1939	Queens Midtown, 1949
Brooklyn Battery, 1950	Throgs Neck, 1961
Verrazano Narrows, 1964	Robert Moses Causeway, 1964

New York City Housing

Stuyvesant Town/
  Peter Cooper Village, 1946
Rochdale Village, 1964

Fresh Meadows, 1947
Cadman Plaza, 1967
Co-op City, 1968

Power Projects

Robert Moses Power Plant,
  St. Lawrence River, 1959

Robert Moses Power Plant,
  Niagara River, 1962

State Parks in Nassau and Suffolk Counties

Heckscher State, 1924
Montauk Point, 1924
Valley Stream, 1925
Belmont Lake, 1926
Gilgo Beach, 1928
Captree, 1930
Connetquot, 1963

Hither Hills, 1924
Wildwood, 1925
Sunken Meadow, 1926
Jones Beach, 1927
Orient Beach, 1929
Caumsett, 1961
Robert Moses, 1964

New York City Parks in Brooklyn and Queens

Alley Pond, 1935
Brookville, 1964
Corona
Dyker Beach
Jacob Riis
Marine, 1936
Rockaway

Astoria, 1936
Corlears Hook, 1939
Cunningham
Forest
Juniper Valley, 1937
Owl's Head, 1937
Spring Creek

(Dates, where known, are of openings.)

Introduction

On June 10 and 11, 1988, the Long Island Studies Institute at Hofstra University convened its third scholarly conference, with the object of observing the centennial of Robert Moses' birth. Our intent was not to examine Moses the Power Broker, but rather Moses the Planner and Moses the Builder, especially for the impact his planning and building had on the Long Island environment.

There was little that Robert Moses achieved in the way of development that did not affect Long Island, whether through the suburban spread that followed the trails of his parkways, or the accessibility to New York City made possible by his bridges and tunnels, which conveyed suburbanites to their businesses. By choosing to focus on Moses' role as a designer of the planned environment we had hoped to establish whether or not his innovations partook of a wider tradition of planning in America, a tradition perhaps best exemplified by the work of Frederick Law Olmsted in the nineteenth century. The reality, however, is that the work of Robert Moses cannot be encompassed within any tradition, for it is marked by uniqueness.

In the Director's Message which appeared in the conference program, I hinted at that uniqueness by pointing out that Moses was not just a builder of bridges, nor simply a designer of parks; he was these *and* a designer of parkways, *and* an environmentalist, as well as an enemy of those who advocated mass transit, and of those who sought to introduce to Long Island great sprawling tracts of suburban housing. He also had the power to carry through in most of these areas, and therein lay the secret of his uniqueness, for no other city planner had ever had at his disposal so much of the machinery of power as did Robert Moses.

And so, whether we wished to or not, we found ourselves, inevitably, dealing with the subject of Robert Moses and political power.

At the conference banquet, Robert A. Caro, Moses'

biographer, expressed two hopes to the conferees, first, that they would not forget that Robert Moses, planner of the built environment, was "a dreamer and an idealist, a visionary, a very courageous idealist," and, second, that they would not neglect "the human cost" of Robert Moses' building. In subsequently demonstrating the progress from vision to cost, Caro, too, returned to the subject of political power.

Explaining his preference for the writing of biography, Caro, who is presently engaged in the creation of a three-volume biography of Lyndon B. Johnson, made it clear that his interest lay not in telling a life story, but in examining "the great forces that shaped the times in which [his subjects] lived, particularly the political power." "Why am I so interested in political power? Because in a democracy political power shapes all our individual lives." The fact that Moses, unlike Lyndon B. Johnson, never held elected office, yet exercised wide and long-term political power, made him doubly fascinating to Caro.

At the time of the conference, the Caro biography, *The Power Broker: Robert Moses and the Fall of New York,* had dominated not only Moses scholarship, but the field of contemporary biography for fourteen years. Since its publication in 1974 it has maintained an intimidating and daunting presence in the minds of all who have read even a portion of its 1100 pages. Hailed by all but the staunchest of Moses' supporters, it has commanded attention from prize committees (Caro was awarded both the Pulitzer and Parkman prizes), and has set the standard for the writing of modern urban history. And it has portrayed Robert Moses as a supreme master of the uses of political power, a ruthless manipulator of human lives in the pursuit of his own grand designs.

It was this portrayal of Moses that Professor Kenneth Jackson, keynoter of the conference, chose to challenge. Jackson, Mellon Professor of History and Social Sciences at Columbia University, and recipient of the Francis Parkman Award and the Bancroft Prize for *Crabgrass Frontier: The Suburbanization of America,* took as his charge "the attempt to place Robert Moses on a broader canvas and in a larger regional and national framework." In essence, he claimed, his argument is "that a more temperate and moderate view of Robert Moses is closer in accord with the evidence." Jackson's support of this claim forms the substance of

Introduction 15

his remarks, which head this volume. Grouped immediately after his call for a re-evaluation are those conference presentations which, by their questioning of some of Caro's assumptions and conclusions, point the way toward further inquiries, or provide insight into lesser known sides of Moses' varied career.

A second group of essays examines the intricacies of political power as they came to bear on particular Moses projects, and a third looks at Queens County for evidence of Moses' designing hand. Another grouping allows for a concentration on Nassau and Suffolk, tracing the before and after of those counties relative to Moses' comprehensive planning.

Included in this section is a transcript of a talk given by Moses in 1974 in which he not only recalls the building of Jones Beach, but defends himself against many who attempted to block that project or who remained critics after its completion. Though Moses often found himself in the position of having to defend his actions, this particular defense, delivered to a historical society on Long Island's south shore (Freeport), came long after the facts of the battle for Jones Beach, and so he was able to speak from a position of strength and of seemingly unimpeachable correctness of judgment. Perhaps the most valuable aspect of the address is Moses' presentation of himself as the visionary, a role which, to his thinking, he never abandoned.

Finally, there is a brief look at Robert Moses' influence as it is revealed in such disparate aspects of design as park furnishings and the creation, out of Long Island's natural environment, of a Mosesland vacation area for harried New Yorkers.

A similar stylistic influence was exerted in the field of architecture, for Moses personally passed on the design plans of each of the architects who worked on his building projects. The conference featured an exhibit by Peter Kaufman of the public works of Aymar Embury II in New York City and Long Island. Embury was one of Moses' favorite architects; he was also the architect for the first buildings to constitute a Hofstra campus. We have included an edited version of the catalog description along with some photographs of Embury's work.

A Roundtable Discussion at the conference brought together such notables of the Office of New York State Parks as its Commissioner, Orin Lehman, and the then-Commision Chairman of the Long Island State Parks, Myron H. Blumenfeld. The length of experience represented by these two dignitaries was complemented by the presence of Peter L. Kramer, who chairs the Parks Advisory Commission and who has contributed to this volume a fine essay on the day-to-day operations of Jones Beach, and David Oats, whose early contact with Robert Moses, described here in an absorbing personal essay, resulted in a lasting interest in the Flushing Meadows park.

Papers included in the conference presentations but not in this volume are on deposit in the Long Island Studies Institute, Hofstra University. They are Iris Berman's study of "The Impact of the Robert Moses Power Plant on Industrial Location," Michael P. McCarthy's questioning of influence in the design of Jones Beach which suggests the work of Daniel Burnham as a possible source, Fred W. Viehe's essay on "Joseph Jensen, the Robert Moses of California," and Marc A. Weiss' discussion of "The American Real Estate Industry and National Housing Policy." Cyril Galvin emphasized the engineering feat that made the construction of the "Fire Island Jetty" such a success, Gary Hammond traced the development of Bethpage State Park from it prior status as a private estate, and Marilyn Weigold provided insight into "Robert Moses, Bridgebuilder."

Two other presentations not included are of particular interest to scholars working on Moses' public papers. Leonora Gidlund described the collection of materials from Moses' term as Commissioner of the New York Parks Department, 1934 through 1960, which are available at the Municipal Archives, a Division of the New York City Department of Records and Information Services. George Tselos did the same for the papers, largely official and personal correspondence, of Robert Moses contained in the collection of the Rare Books and Manuscripts Division of The New York Public Library. The inclusive dates of the collection are 1912–1980. Both of these presentations are available in the Long Island Studies Institute.

The choice of title, "Robert Moses, Single-Minded Genius," for the collection of essays derives from the opening statement of Kenneth Jackson's argument where he describes Moses as "the single-minded genius who molded New York City into a twentieth-century metropolis." The exact nature of the objective of this single-mindedness remains in doubt so long as there are diverging views of Moses' genius. Robert Caro has held the field

Introduction 17

for a long while with his view of a single objective, political power. Kenneth Jackson and others represented here disagree, as has one of our conferees, Roger Starr, in a *New York Times* editorial of August 18, 1988 where he defended Moses against such charges as racism and "auto-infatuation." Robert Moses also disagreed that his single objective was political power, and in the Jones Beach talk reproduced here he identifies what he no doubt considered his primary objective: "public enterprise." "Here it is in a nutshell," he says, referring to the Jones Beach project, "[A]n example of planned, imaginative, persistent, nonpolitical public enterprise." The time has come for a re-evaluation of Robert Moses and of Robert Caro's Robert Moses. Let it begin here.

Joann P. Krieg

RE-EVALUATING THE POWER BROKER

Collection of Hofstra Museum, HU 84.67
Photograph, copyright, Brian Ballweg

Bust of Robert Moses by George Gach, 1973

Robert Moses and the Planned Environment: A Re-Evaluation*

Kenneth T. Jackson

More than any other person or institution, Robert Moses was the single-minded genius who molded New York City into a twentieth century metropolis. The protean agent of the huge public works project, Moses was the greatest builder in American history and as powerful a non-elected public official as the United States has yet produced. Indeed, he was active and influential, until his death in 1981 at the age of 92, as an expert in the art of expediting the construction of immense structures.

Between 1924 and 1968, Moses conceived and executed public works costing $27 billion (before post-Vietnam War inflation). His was the dominant planning influence during these years in the city and state of New York, an arena and a period that included Governor Alfred E. Smith, Mayor Fiorello LaGuardia, Governor and President Franklin D. Roosevelt, Governor W. Averell Harriman, Senator Robert F. Wagner, Governor Herbert H. Lehman, Governor Thomas E. Dewey, Mayor John V. Lindsay, and Governor Nelson Rockefeller, not to mention the leaders of the political machines or the bankers of Wall Street. Indeed, in the field of public works, Moses' impact was as great as the rest of them combined. In addition to increasing the number of neighborhood playgrounds from 119 to 374, Moses planted more than 2 million trees, and opened Jones Beach and Orchard Beach in his first decade as Park Commissioner. Moses was responsible for virtually every parkway, expressway, and public housing complex in the city, as well as the Brooklyn-Battery Tunnel (he had planned a bridge there instead); the Henry Hudson, Bronx-Whitestone, Cross Bay, Throgs Neck, Verrazano-Narrows, Marine

---

*Keynote Address for the Conference on "Robert Moses and the Planned Environment," Hofstra University, June 10–11, 1988.

Parkway, and Triborough Bridges; Lincoln Center for the Performing Arts; Shea Stadium; and both the 1939 and 1964 World's Fairs.

Moses transformed the city. In the 1930s, for example, the waterfront along the Upper West Side of Manhattan was a six-mile long wasteland. Although called Riverside Park, the area was scarred by rotting timbers, mounds of untreated garbage, and tarpaper squatter settlements. Ten years later, the area had been transformed. The railroad tracks were covered with tennis courts, lawns, promenades, playgrounds, and the nation's first controlled-access parkway within a major city stretched northward from 72nd Street beyond the George Washington Bridge all the way to Riverdale in the Bronx. Whether or not Moses deserves the credit for first envisaging such transformation, he was the individual who managed to transform a dream into reality.

Moses left his mark not only on New York, but on the entire nation. Many of the designers and administrators of the Bureau of Public Roads and later the Interstate Highway system had originally been trained as "Moses men," and they remained disciples of their former chief. Lewis Mumford, a consistent opponent of the big roads philosophy, has written that: "In the twentieth century the influence of Robert Moses on the cities of America was greater than that of any other person." As was said of Sir Christopher Wren in St. Paul's Cathedral in London: *Si monumentum requiris, circumspice,* or, If you would see his monument, look about you.

This Hofstra University conference is the first of what will probably be many observances of the centennial of Moses' birth, and it calls attention to the extraordinary range of his achievements. Indeed, any one of a half a hundred Moses projects would represent the crowning achievement in a career of distinction.

Unlike most great men, Robert Moses was the subject during his lifetime of a great book. Serialized in four issues of *The New Yorker* even before it was published by Alfred A. Knopf in 1974, *The Power Broker* became a best seller in hardcover and in paperback, and it has been a special favorite of college students. Indeed, I have required it in practically every class I have taught for the past fourteen years. Superbly comprehensive and engagingly written, it won critical as well as popular plaudits, and earned Robert A. Caro both the Francis Parkman and Pulitzer Prizes.

After almost fifteen years, however, it is now time for a reappraisal of the career of Robert Moses, and the Hofstra conference brings together more than a score of scholars who have been examining various phases of the Power Broker's career. As the keynote speaker for this gathering, I take as my charge not the explication of a particular incident, but rather the attempt to place Robert Moses on a broader canvas and in a larger regional and national framework. Essentially, I will argue that a more temperate and moderate view of Robert Moses is closer in accord with the evidence. As examples of this proposition, I should like to examine the evidence in three areas, transportation, housing, and racism.

Transportation

The Power Broker suggests that Moses was not only responsible for most of the road network around New York City, but that the metropolitan region was peculiarly directed toward a rubber-tire environment. Caro further asserts that Moses was influential in redirecting public funds away from subways and buses, and in killing the nickel fare in 1948.

Obviously, there is some truth to this charge. One need only consider the various expressways which Moses masterminded and built—the Interborough, Grand Central, Belt, Van Wyck, Prospect, Clearview, Brooklyn-Queens, Gowanus, Whitestone, Northern State, Wantagh State, Meadowbrook, Long Island, Southern State, Major Deegan, Bruckner, and Cross Bronx Expressways, not to mention the Hutchinson River Parkway, the West Side Highway, the FDR Drive, the Henry Hudson Parkway, and the Harlem River Drive. Caro agreed with the position espoused most prominently by Jane Jacobs (with which I happen also to agree) that new roads often exacerbate rather than solve traffic problems.*

In considering the role of Robert Moses in redirecting transportation priorities in the New York area, however, it is important to remember that the great builder was swimming with

---

*See Jane Jacobs, *The Death and Life of Great American Cities* (New York: Random House, 1961). Editor's note.

the tide of history. During most of his lifetime, the operative question was not whether to build highways or subways; almost everyone other than Lewis Mumford believed that the automobile was the greatest invention since the wheel. Rather, the essential questions were what kinds of highways should be built and where would they go.

In a comparative sense, what is striking about the New York metropolitan region is not the number of its expressways, but rather their absence; not the existence of traffic, but rather the observation that congestion in Gotham is no worse than in smaller cities like Atlanta, Houston, or Los Angeles; not the presence of a rubber tire mentality, but rather the fact that per capita gasoline consumption in the New York area is now, and has long been, easily the lowest in the United States.

All this is despite what Robert Moses did. Six decades ago, when Moses was only beginning his incredible career, about 20 percent of American mass transit riders were in the New York metropolitan region; in 1988, about 35 percent were in the same area. Thus, from a national perspective, what needs to be explained is exactly the opposite of what Caro proposed. How has the New York public transportation system survived when those of the rest of the nation have collapsed? Why have automobile ownership and gasoline consumption here remained so far below that of other cities?

It is true, as Caro alleges, that Moses did nothing to save the nickel fare. But Moses was not in charge of public transportation, and could have been expected to fight in the political arena for those projects for which he did have responsibility. Moreover, as most transit experts now agree, the nickel fare should have been abandoned in the 1920s, not the 1940s. Because the fare box could not pay for normal operating expenses, let alone for capital improvements, the subway system could not make the improvements that might have avoided the deterioration which plagued it after World War II. Finally, we should remember that Mayor Fiorello LaGuardia was a vigorous opponent of rail transit and personally endorsed the ripping up of Manhattan trolley tracks in the 1930s.

Public Housing

The Power Broker makes several assertions about public housing that may be revised as additional evidence is unearthed by other researchers. Robert Caro charges, for example, that the New York projects were disproportionately large and that Moses cut corners in construction because he had little regard for the needs of the poor. As to size, one might point out that the Robert Taylor Homes in Chicago dwarf any of the projects in New York, and that Newark, New Jersey, has always had a larger percentage of public housing than its larger neighbor to the east. As to the assertion that Moses left doors off closets and allowed elevators to stop only on alternate floors, the rejoinder might be made that the original legislation creating public housing, as well as subsequent appropriations, discriminated against high cost locations like New York by limiting the amount of money that could be spent on individual units. This occurred because southern lawmakers, who were biased against New York anyway, were never eager to see Washington largesse lavished on other regions. They fought for, and won, stipulations which effectively tied Moses' hands.

Given the financial constraints which have always obtained in the construction of public housing in the United States, what is remarkable about the New York City projects is not their shoddiness, but their quality. In city after city in the United States, from Boston to St. Louis to Newark, public housing has fallen into disrepair and has even been blown up by local authorities. Despite severe housing shortages in each of those cities, many needy citizens have simply refused to move into units that are unsafe, unsanitary, and inconvenient.

How different is the situation in New York City. Indeed, there are no abandoned public housing structures in New York, and, in comparison to most other big cities—Chicago is a particularly horrifying example—what is unique about the projects in New York is their quality, their desirability, and their popularity. In the South Bronx, where the private housing stock has declined by perhaps a third in the past two decades, the public housing units dominate the landscape and provide powerful evidence that government can provide a better housing alternative for the poor.

Racism

Perhaps the most damning indictment that Caro brings against Moses is the charge that he was a racist—a racist in thought as well as in action, a man whose prejudices shaped his behavior and his policies during his many decades as a public servant.

There is deep within the soul of most of us a strain of prejudice that lingers in spite of education, experience, and effort. Robert Moses was human, and we may assume that his intellectual and emotional baggage had a dark side.

But the evidence that the Power Broker was unusual in his racism is weak, especially when Moses is considered within his time and place. In 1925, for example, in the middle of Harlem, along 125th Street, there was scarcely a restaurant that would serve a black patron, there was no theater that would accept a black citizen on the main floor, and there was not a single major store that would hire a black clerk. Indeed, there was such obvious discrimination among the larger emporiums that rioting in 1935 and again in 1943 focused on the absence of black salespersons along 125th Street.

Robert Caro makes a number of charges to support his allegations of racism. For one thing, he suggests Moses built the overpasses above the Long Island parkways too low for buses to pass under them. Thus, the only persons able to avail themselves of Jones Beach would be members of the white middle class. The problems with this charge are several. First, the bridges were built at a low height because raising them by even two feet would have doubled their cost. Second, it was possible in the 1930s, as it remains possible in 1988, to get to Jones Beach by public transportation. The price of a ticket no doubt deterred the poor—Coney Island's beach could have been reached for a nickel until after World War II. But racism itself is a charge that requires much more evidence than is offered.

A second assertion of Moses' prejudice concerns the lack of a park along the Hudson River at 125th Street. All up and down the Hudson River, the Power Broker created magnificent open spaces, except of course in the area where blacks lived.

This assertion also lacks convincing proof. For one thing, blacks did not live along the western reaches of 125th Street until long after these decisions were reached. Second, the topography of the land is dramatically different, and lower, from 120th Street to 135th Street where a valley bisects Manhattan Island. Thus, there are alternative explanations for the configuration of Riverside Park other than the assertion that Robert Moses was a racist.

The Destruction of Neighborhoods

Perhaps the strongest indictment of the Power Broker is the charge that he loved the public but disliked people, that he built a city but destroyed its vitality. As in everything else, there is a large measure of truth to this assertion. Moses viewed the metropolis largely as an economic and transportation problem, not as a delicate interplay of families, businesses, and neighborhoods. As much as anyone in the twentieth century, he believed in a suburban rather than an urban ideal. Thus, when he chose the route for an expressway through the city, his perspective was that of a traffic engineer, not a sociologist.

The most damaging example of Moses' disregard for neighborhood priorities was East Tremont in the Bronx, the subject of a particularly powerful section of Caro's book. According to the prevailing interpretation, a vibrant, healthy, working-class, Jewish area was destroyed by the Cross Bronx Expressway and by Moses' unwillingness to consider alternative routes. Quite simply, a huge, eight-lane interstate highway was rammed through the safe and peaceful streets of an idyllic and affordable neighborhood.

The problem with this simplistic explanation is that it is wrong. Of course, East Tremont residents remembered that theirs was a wonderful neighborhood in the early 1950s. As humans, we almost always remember the best things about our former homes. What is more to the point is how their contemporaries living elsewhere viewed East Tremont.

For this purpose, the most objective sources are the Residential Security Maps and accompanying explanations prepared by the Home Owners Loan Corporation (HOLC) a half century ago. As I have indicated in *Crabgrass Frontier: The Suburbanization of the United States*, federal appraisers made judgements about every neighborhood in every city during the

1930s and 1940s. Like other Americans of the time, they were prejudiced in a variety of ways, and they downgraded places that were racially integrated, or occupied by Jews, or, generally densely populated. Thus, the Bronx as a whole suffered at the hands of the Federal Housing Administration and the HOLC.

But there was an element of consistency about the Residential Security Ratings, and some Jewish sections, such as the Grand Concourse, received as high as a "B" rating. Federal appraisers, then, did not always give Jewish sections low ratings.

What is interesting about East Tremont is that it received the lowest score possible both in 1937 and in 1940, the only years for which records are available. These "D" or "Fourth Class" ratings cast doubt on the reminiscences of Caro's informants. Instead, federal appraisers looked at the rent levels, the age and condition of the buildings, the types of jobs held by residents, and the quality of maintenance in the area, and they came up with deteriorated housing, severe overcrowding, and messy streets. Their elaborate evaluation noted that East Tremont was "hazardous" for investment in 1940, fourteen years before construction for the Cross Bronx Expressway tore the neighborhood apart.

For the sake of argument, however, let us assume that East Tremont in 1953 was just as *The Power Broker* described it. A half dozen and more other Bronx neighborhoods, however, suffered similar deterioration and decline, and they were not in the path of the Cross Bronx Expressway. Charlotte Street, for example, the most notorious slum in the United States in the 1970s and 1980s, and the scene of well-publicized campaign visits by Jimmy Carter and Ronald Reagan, is well away from the Cross Bronx Expressway. In other words, even if Robert Moses had redirected the controversial roadway, the likelihood is that East Tremont would have experienced dramatic demographic and economic changes. This is because highway construction has not been the only factor responsible for neighborhood change in the United States. We should exercise caution in ascribing broad changes to any singular causation. Caro would have been on more solid ground if he had pointed out how federal programs and large-scale population shifts played the major role in the decline of East Tremont.

A New Interpretation of Robert Moses

The broad outline of Robert A. Caro's *The Power Broker* may be essentially correct. Robert Moses was hard-working, demanding, arrogant, intelligent, and ruthless, and he rebuilt the greatest city in the world.

Caro's extremely negative view will, however, be modified in coming decades. Basically, Caro fails to put Moses into a broad national context, and he thus attributes too much good and too much evil to this single person. A broader view, for example, would give more attention to the Regional Plan Association, which in fact initially developed the idea of a circumferential highway system for New York in the 1920s, and to the New York Port Authority, which defeated Moses on the issues of airports and bus terminals. Such a view would note that Jones Beach, Riverside Park, and the Throgs Neck Bridge, to take obvious examples, did not spring solely from the mind of Robert Moses. Finally, such a reinterpretation would suggest that the great builder, while never a candidate for the Humanitarian of the Year Award, was no more anti-semitic or racist than most of his contemporaries.

The achievement of Robert Moses was that, as Andrew Haswell Green, William Cullen Bryant, and Frederick Law Olmsted adapted New York City to the needs of the nineteenth century, so he, more than any other person, adapted the great metropolis to the requirements of the twentieth century. While few people would endorse everything Moses did, it is not possible to say merely that New York would have been a different place without Moses: it would have been a worse place without Moses. While we may deplore an American transportation policy that subsidizes the automobile and squanders the earth's precious oil, it is, unfortunately, a fact that no modern city, anywhere, can function without a well developed road network.

The achievement of Robert Moses can best be put into perspective when we consider how poorly we are currently preparing for the remainder of the twentieth century, let alone for the twenty-first century. Since Moses lost power in 1968, New York City has built no new bridges, no new highways, virtually no new public housing projects, no new performing arts centers, and no new beaches. Its parks have deteriorated, and its infrastructure is crumbling. The sewage treatment plant on the west side of Manhattan, which was under construction when I moved to New York in 1968, is still unfinished, twenty years and a billion dollars later. Similarly, the Second Avenue subway and the third water tunnel threaten to drag into the next century.

Robert Moses made possible New York's ascendency to world primacy in the twentieth century. If another Robert Moses does not appear, however, New York is not likely to retain its exalted status in the face of fierce competition from Tokyo, Sao Paulo, Mexico City, and Los Angeles.

Some Reflections on Moses and his Biographer

*Jameson W. Doig**

> I don't agree with you about Caro because a considerable part of his stuff is false and malicious along with much that is painstaking and accurate. He is a dead duck. (Robert Moses, letter to the author, 20 July 1978.)

There is no question that Robert Caro's book is a valuable contribution to the literature on Robert Moses, on the development of the New York region, and on the political process generally. Like many who teach courses covering these subjects, I assign portions of *The Power Broker* to my students. Despite Moses' sometime wish, Caro is not "a dead duck."

Moreover, Caro provides the reader not only with a perceptive and well-written narrative, but with detailed information on his sources. His endnotes often allow the reader to determine what books, unpublished documents, and interviews contributed to his analysis, page by page, and in many cases the skeptic can pursue descriptions and assertions to the original sources. For this as well as for his rich narrative we are in his debt.

There is a third gift which Caro brings us in *The Power Broker*, a gift of alloyed benefit. Caro brings passion to his story—a passion that catches and holds the reader's attention, a passion that at times overwhelms the author's probing intelligence. The great biographer of Henry James, Leon Edel, warns us that

> the relation of the biographer to the subject is the very core of the biographical enterprise. Idealization of the hero or the heroine blinds the writer of lives to the meaning of the materials. Hatred or animosity does the same. . . . If there

---

*These reflections were originally the closing paragraphs of my paper, "Airports, Bus Terminals, and Great Bridges," prepared for the Hofstra Conference, June 1988. (See pp. 57–67).

ensues an emotional involvement on the part of the biographer he or she must be reminded that love is blind.[1]

To this reader, Caro's interpretation shows much emotional involvement, and a curious mixture of adulation and repulsion. One example of this mixture, strongly tilted toward awe, can be found in the section of *The Power Broker* entitled "The Lust for Power:"

> To compare the works of Robert Moses to the works of man, one has to compare them not to the works of individual men but to the combined total work of an era. . . . He was, for the greatest city in the Western world, the city shaper, the only city shaper. . . . He is comparable not to the works of any man or group of men or even generations of men. In the shaping of New York, Robert Moses was comparable only to some elemental force of nature. But if in the shaping of New York Robert Moses was an elemental force, he was also a blind force: blind and deaf, blind and deaf to reason, to argument, to new ideas, to any ideas except his own.[2]

As Leon Edel suggests, we should be wary of such judgments, hurled down in such a voice. They are likely to obscure truth as much as they reveal it. Because of Caro's passion toward Moses, it is likely that careful studies of specific cases will find Moses less influential—and perhaps less abusive, less despising of others—than does Caro's giant tome.

And on the broad and important issue of whether Moses was *the* dominant force in shaping New York and its region, Caro is, I think, almost certainly wrong. He has not carefully thought through the complex casual forces that shape an urban society. It is likely that Robert Moses was as much a captive as he was a shaper of the economic and other social forces that have determined the rise and decline of American cities and suburbs in the twentieth century.[3]

NOTES

1. Leon Edel, *Writing Lives* (New York: W. W. Norton, 1984), p. 14.
2. Robert Caro, *The Power Broker* (New York: Knopf, 1974), p. 830.
3. On these casual patterns, see for example Robert Wood, *1400 Governments: the Political Economy of the New York Metropolitan Region*

(Cambridge, Mass.: Harvard University Press, 1961); J. W. Doig and M. N. Danielson, "From the Firm Ground of Result and Fact to the Tossing Sea of Cause and Theory," *Policy Studies Journal,* Summer 1980, pp. 852–861.

Robert Caro's Moses: A Historian's Critique

George Stevens

More than the biography it claims to be, Robert Caro's *The Power Broker* is an epic of the worlds greatest city and the man who contributed so much to its present contours. Its hero, Robert Moses, is a figure whose intelligence and superhuman energy can only be described as Napoleonic in stature, his ability to GET THINGS DONE the stuff of which legends are made.

"In the twentieth century," observed Lewis Mumford—no less critic of Moses than Caro but one not given to hyperbole—"the influence of Robert Moses on the cities of America was greater than that of any other person."[1] Caro makes the same point, but in his characteristic style:

> Robert Moses was unquestionably America's most prolific physical creator. He was America's greatest builder.... He was, for the greatest city in the Western world, the city shaper, the only city shaper. In sheer physical impact on New York and the entire New York metropolitan region, he is comparable not to the works of any man or group of men or even generations of men. In the shaping of New York, Robert Moses was comparable only to some elemental force of nature (Caro, pp. 10; 830).

The list of the Master Builder's works which appears earlier in the volume reveals that Caro's claims are not merely rhetorical exaggeration. To make certain that the significance and magnitude of his hero's achievements are fully grasped, Caro provides such additional information as these:

—Regarding Manhattan landfills—

He changed its very shape . . . and . . . expanded and transformed its physical contours, adding to Manhattan Island alone an area as large as the island from river to river between 59th and 86th Streets (Caro, p. 508).

—Regarding the Triborough Bridge—

Its anchorages, the masses of concrete in which its cables would be embedded, would be as big as any pyramid built by an Egyptian pharoah, its roadway wider than the widest roadways built by the Caesars of Rome. To construct those anchorages and to pave those roadways . . . would require enough concrete to pave a four lane highway from New York to Philadelphia. . . . The amount of human energy that would be expended in its construction gives some idea of its immensity: more than five thousand men would be working on the site (Caro, pp. 386–87).

—Regarding the Brooklyn Battery Tunnel—

The tile used to line it would have tiled 4,500 bathrooms; to ventilate it . . . air would have to be driven through ducts at the velocity of a Force Twelve hurricane, and the fans which drove that air would consume daily as much electricity as is used daily by a small city (Caro, p. 844).

In addition to these engineering feats, in 1919 Moses drew up the plan which completely reorganized the administrative machinery of New York's state government. Walter Lippman called this "one of the greatest achievements in modern American politics." Caro concurs. "It may be," he writes, "that this achievement is at least the equal of any of the others" (Caro, p. 262).

* * *

Despite the enormity of these accomplishments the Robert Moses who emerges from the pages of *The Power Broker* is far from heroic. One of Moses' chief personality characteristics—arrogance—was well suited to the role of villain. "Robert Moses," states Caro, "had no respect for anyone's opinion but his own" (Caro, p. 484). This arrogance coupled with the power he wielded made it possible for another Mosaic personality trait to emerge—ruthlessness.

"If you know," a prominent judge once remarked, "that every time you get in a guy's way, he's going to kick you in the balls, you make pretty damn sure you don't get in the way—right?" "Any time someone got in Moses' way," writes Caro, "Moses kicked him in the balls" (Caro, p. 507). While the kicks were most often figurative, they could also be literal. During the 30s and 40s news circulated among New York political insiders of Moses' physical attacks on those who disagreed with him. If the kicks didn't work, Moses had another tool that could achieve the desired result. Using his staff to compile dossiers on friends and foes alike, Robert Moses, states Caro, "was a pioneer in McCarthyism, twenty years before McCarthy" (Caro, p. 472).

His methods and even his vision of society were essentially anti-democratic. If he disregarded and intimidated men who should have been his peers, Robert Moses' attitude toward the lower classes, especially the non-white lower classes, can be summed up in a single word: disdain. This was readily reflected in his actions. His policies at the recreation facilities under his control—Jones Beach and city swimming pools for example—were designed to deny blacks full enjoyment of them. More revealingly, says Caro, "Robert Moses built 255 playgrounds in New York City during the 1930s. He built one playground in Harlem" (Caro, p. 510).

In the area of public housing Moses' disdain and insensitivity were further manifested. There should be no frills, but only a roof over the heads of people too lazy or too ignorant to provide one for themselves. "Among the frills Moses objected to," remarks Caro, "were: covers on toilet bowls, doors on closets" (Caro, p. 758).

Moses' lack of concern for the lower orders is glaringly evident in the clearance projects necessary for his expressways and Title I programs. "When you operate in an overbuilt metropolis," Moses once remarked, "you have to hack your way with a meat ax" (Caro, p. 849). The swinging of that ax was something Moses appeared to relish, and as he cleaved his way through the densely populated city viable neighborhoods were destroyed and thousands upon thousands of people were displaced. "To build his highways," Caro observes:

> Moses threw out of their homes 250,000 persons—more people than lived in Albany or Chattanooga, or in Spokane, Tacoma, Duluth, Akron, Baton Rouge, Mobile, Nashville or Sacramento. He tore out the hearts of a score of neighborhoods, communities the size of small cities, communities that had been lively, friendly places to live, the vital parts of the city that made New York a home to its people (Caro, p. 19).

The characteristics of the evacuees are quite revealing. According to the 1950 census 12% of New York City's population was non-white. However, 37% of those evacuated by Moses during that decade were non-white. Moreover, in 1950 an income of $4,083 was deemed necessary for a family of four to live decently but only 25% of the evacuees earned $4,083 or more and an alarming 20% actually had incomes of less than $2,000 per year. "Moses," says Caro accusingly, "was throwing out of their homes precisely those people who were least able to find new homes" (Caro, p. 968).

Because of the power he wielded, the priorities of Robert Moses became those of the city and the metropolitan region. However, those priorities were not designed to meet the needs of the people. Moses' goal was to ring the city and its surrounding environs with highways and bridges, and although he achieved spectacular success in these areas he did so at the expense of other municipal services. During his years of power, education, libraries, fire houses and hospitals were, relatively speaking, neglected. Moreover, Moses not only neglected mass transit but actually made its situation worse. It is for this that Caro reserves some of his sharpest barbs.

For thirty years (1935–1955) Moses' policies had emphasized highways at the expense of mass transit. But, says Caro, "so superbly engineered and maintained had the system been previously that it took years of systematic neglect to take its toll" (Caro, p. 932). The year 1955, however, marked the "Point of No Return" for mass transit in New York and the Metropolitan Region. In that year the Triborough Bridge and Tunnel Authority and the Port Authority announced a joint program whereby the authorities' surplus revenues would be invested in a massive program of bridge and highway construction rather than in mass transit. Caro readily summarizes the consequences of this choice: "When Robert Moses came to power in New York in 1934, the city's mass transportation was probably the best in the world. When he left power in 1968, it was quite possibly the worst" (Caro, p. 933).

If Robert Moses is the chief actor and antagonist in the piece, there is another more subtle villain that Caro takes to task—the press. "The Press," remarked Paul Kern an aide to Mayor LaGuardia, " . . . had babied him like a spoiled child. He couldn't do anything wrong in their eyes. They made him a myth." Having created the myth the press gave Moses a free ride for most of his career. "The press," observes Caro, "which was turning him into a legend in his own time had scant space to spare for his critics" (Caro, p. 462).

In Caro's view Moses and the media shared much in common. If he operated from an independent power base and was accountable to no one, the same could be said of the press. If he exhibited a decided class bias, so too did the press. Examples of this abound throughout the book, the most poignant of which involved the battle to seek an alternate route for the Cross Bronx Expressway, a battle to save thousands of working class homes. As Lillian Edelstein (a Bronx housewife who is one of Caro's heroes) and her supporters poured their energy into the fight, the city's three most influential dailies either ignored it or provided coverage slanted toward Moses. "The fate of poor people," Caro acidly remarks, "had never been news in New York City, it was still not news" (Caro, pp. 869, 979, 990).

In the fifties the romance between Moses and the media began to cool. However, this was not because of the dislocation and suffering of tens of thousands of lower and working class New Yorkers caused by Moses' policies. The issues which chiefly contributed to the estrangement again revealed the class bias of the press. In 1956, Moses proposed to build a parking lot near the Tavern on the Green in Central Park. This would destroy a playground used largely, if not exclusively, by the children of middle class parents. In 1959, Moses and his aides engaged in an effort to curtail Joseph Papp's Shakespeare in the Park program. While Papp's performances were free and open to the public, their continuance was still largely a middle class concern. It was these two issues that the press seized upon to begin its long overdue critical examination of Robert Moses. While the playground and the Board were unquestionably deserving of attention, they certainly were not as worthy as the plight of lower class New Yorkers when Moses swung his meat ax (Caro, pp. 986–88, 1026–39).

How was Robert Moses able to attain and exercise the influence he did for so long a time? His story is most certainly not that of a Horatio Alger hero. Born into very favorable circumstances to a German-Jewish family of considerable means, he never wanted for anything. Doing his undergraduate work at Yale and graduate studies at Oxford, he received an education well suited to one who would exercise authority. Furthermore, and most significantly, his family's wealth afforded him the luxury that made it possible for him to take non-paying or low paying government positions early in his career. This had two important consequences. First, it allowed him to become acquainted with the levers of power and the players who operated them, most notably Belle Moskowitz and Al Smith. Second, the fact that Moses received very little, if any, remuneration for his efforts helped establish his reputation as a disinterested, self-sacrificing, scrupulously honest public servant whose sole concern was the commonwealth. This would contribute substantially to making him a legend in the eyes of the press and, by extension, in the eyes of much of the public as well. The media's role in Moses' accumulation and exercise of power was, in Caro's view, of the utmost importance.

Favorable social circumstances do not a power broker make; individual agency was not without its role. Robert Moses possessed extraordinary energy, remarkable stamina and an intelligence that was impressive when measured by any criteria. All these, especially the last named, contributed significantly to Moses' acquisition and exercise of power.

During the twenties Moses came to be acknowledged as "The Best Bill Drafter in Albany." Not only was this obviously a reflection of his shrewdness and intelligence but it proved a substantial source of his influence. Buried deep within those masterfully crafted bills were clauses designed to augment the power of Robert Moses, power which once codified would be virtually unassailable (Caro, pp. 172–77).

The Public Authority device was originally created in England during the reign of Queen Elizabeth. Three hundred years later, the concept was still novel in the United States. During the Great Depression Moses' insightful and restless intelligence seized upon the device as a potential source of immense power. Consequently he created numerous public authorities the most important of which was the Triborough Bridge and Tunnel Authority. "His authorities," writes Caro:

> ... had not only all the powers of "bodies corporate" but many of the powers of "bodies politic"—including bodies

> politic that were sovereign states. . . . They had, in fact, some powers that sovereign states—at least the sovereign state of New York—did not. They could let contracts without positive bidding. Their officials could be removed only for cause; they were immune from the pleasure of the Governor . . . now he [Moses] needed executive support no longer . . . the authority enabling acts had given him resources of money and power independent of Governors and Mayors. Their approval was no longer required . . . his authorities would do what he wanted done (Caro, pp. 628–30).

During a career that spanned five decades Robert Moses acquired an almost mythic reputation for his ability to get things done. Not only did Moses conceive public works on a scale previously unknown but his boundless energy, painstaking attention to detail, and ruthless drive invariably caused those projects to be completed on or ahead of schedule. This made him practically indispensable to elected officials. "Elections," comments Caro, "come every two years, or four, and the official who wants reelection needs a record of accomplishment on which to run." Moses' parks, highways and bridges were highly visible achievements. Consequently elected officials interested in enhancing their chances for continuance in office heaped on him more and more responsibilities, which carried with them the grant of ever greater power (Caro, pp. 315–16).

At the height of his career Robert Moses simultaneously occupied twelve different city and state appointive posts. As a master of the game of patronage, he used those posts to further augment his influence. Contractors, trucking concerns, banks, law firms, insurance brokers and labor leaders all paid him tribute. Moses had created an extensive empire and only the master builder wore the crown.

The Power Broker is quite simply a magnificent intellectual accomplishment. Robert Caro displays an enviable breadth of learning and knowledge, and consequently the book contains a wealth of fascinating information which any reader will find stimulating. One feels somewhat guilty raising criticisms about such a marvelous piece of work. From the perspective of the historian, however, *The Power Broker* is far from flawless.

Over the past several years history has increasingly become the study of people rather than persons. Though not denying the efficacy of individual agency, historians have focused their analysis on social process. They have come to see institutional, demographic, economic, social, and environmental factors as the crucial elements in historical development. By contrast, the Robert Moses who emerges from *The Power Broker* seemingly operates in a vacuum as a kind of *deus ex machina* imposing his will, his vision, and his values on a pliant and passive metroplitan region. There is a problem with this. Put simply, the Moses who appears in this book is in many respects ahistorical. Caro tends to assign sole responsibility to Moses for problems whose causes were quite complex and which had deep historical roots. Examples of this abound throughout the book.

One of Caro's themes is that the policies of Robert Moses were most unfair to non-whites. The implication is that Robert Moses was a racist (which is probably true) who, because of his power, influence, and forcefulness, was able to impose his racism on the city's and region's construction policies. What this view overlooks is that these years, which coincided with the majority of Moses' career, witnessed some of the most intense racism in the history of the United States.

It was a time when a legal system of segregation prevailed in the South—a system which, according to the historian C. Vann Woodward, "could hardly find a counterpart short of the latitudes of India and South Africa."[2] It was a time when the policies of the Federal Housing Administration openly encouraged segregation.[3] Closer to home, it was a time when Levittown systematically excluded blacks; a time when in New York City blacks were unwelcome and unseen outside of their residential neighborhoods— except in menial capacities; a time when the Rev. Adam Clayton Powell, Jr., had to lead a boycott of Harlem retail establishments to force merchants to hire black sales personnel. Rather than imposing his racism on an unsuspecting city, as Caro's argument implies, Moses' policies were a reflection of one of American society's most ingrained prejudices.

Another instance of Caro's lack of perspective can be seen in what is arguably the most well known and widely discussed section of *The Power Broker*, those chapters dealing with the construction of the Cross Bronx Expressway (Caro, pp. 839–94). It is in these pages that Moses gleefully and ruthlessly cleaves his way through the overbuilt metropolis and, in the process, willfully and unnecessarily destroys a viable urban neighborhood while insensitively displacing thousands of families. While Moses was certainly less than tactful and maybe even ruthless, Caro's analysis fails to mention other significant factors. The role played by policies of the Federal government in making Moses' actions possible is essentially overlooked. The fact that the same process of highway building and neighborhood gutting was occurring all over the country in cities as diverse as Syracuse, New York, and Detroit, Michigan is all but ignored.[4]

A final and most pertinent example of the limitations of Caro's point of view is manifested in the blame he assigns to Moses for destroying mass transit in the metropolitan region and contributing to suburban sprawl particularly on Long Island (Caro, pp. 895–958). While Moses' policies may have contributed to developments, they did not operate independently.

With the rise of industrialism and the industrial city in the nineteenth century, a transformation took place in the popular view of urban life. This change contributed significantly to the development of suburbia. Sam Bass Warner, Jr., in his classic study, *Streetcar Suburbs,* makes this point when he speaks of the growing influence of the rural ideal in nineteenth-century America. "The rural ideal," he writes:

> ... was an attitude which had always contained the notion of escape from city restraints, organizations and objects. The city's ways and forms were conceived of as too artificial and of the wrong quality to support a moral life... The attraction of the rural ideal and the continued press of industrialization and immigration turned the middle class against city living as it had been know in the past ... the rural ideal ... encouraged the dispersal of the urban population.[5]

The rise of industrial capitalism also contributed to the privatization of family life, a life that could best be lived in the private detached house. "This single family dwelling," writes Kenneth Jackson, "became a paragon of middle class housing, the most visible symbol of having arrived at a fixed place in society the goal to which every decent family aspired."[6] As population grew and density increased, the only place where most middle class people could realize their dream of independent home-ownership was outside the traditional city. This obviously had a significant impact on the development of suburbs.

In the nineteenth and early twentieth centuries, suburban

expansion was limited by access to public transportation. During the first third of the present century, however, this limitation was effectively removed with the arrival of the automobile as an item of mass consumption. Coupled with the availability of cheap fuel, the automobile further stimulated the rise of suburban living. "No other invention," writes Jackson:

> ... has altered urban form more than the internal combustion engine. . . . Before 1920 developable real estate had to be located within walking distance of public transit. After 1920 suburbanization began to require a new character as residential development multiplied.[7]

In addition to the factors already mentioned, the policies of the Federal government played an important part in suburban development and in the decline of mass transit. This can be seen in two areas. First, Federal Housing Administration policies, Jackson points out, favored "new residential developments on the edges of metropolitan areas, to the neglect of core cities."[8] Second, the Interstate Highway Act of 1956, he observes, "helped continue the downward spiral of public trasportation and virtually guaranteed that future . . . growth would perpetuate a centerless sprawl." Revealingly, 75% of Federal expenditures for transportation since World War II was for highways whereas only 1% went to urban mass transit.[9]

The rise of industrial capitalism, the privatization of family life, the attractiveness of the rural ideal, America's love affair with the automobile and the detached house, the role of Federal policy, the development of the subdivision—all major influences in contributing to patterns of settlement in the United States—antedated and were independent of the will of Robert Moses. But these very significant factors are obscured in Caro's analysis.

The point is that the master builder and his policies were much more a product of a historical process than *The Power Broker* indicates. At least as much as he shaped them, Robert Moses reflected his times.

NOTES

1. Robert A. Caro, *The Power Broker: Robert Moses and the Fall of New York City* (New York.: Alfred A. Knopf, 1947), p. 12. Further references to

this volume are contained within the text.

2. C. Vann Woodward, *The Strange Career of Jim Crow,* Third Revised Edition (New York.: Oxford Univ. Press, 1974), p. 101.

3. Kenneth T. Jackson, *Crabgrass Frontier: The Suburbanization of the United States* (New York: Oxford Univ. Press, 1985), pp. 208-09.

4. On the impact of Interstate 75 on Detroit, see *The Wall Street Journal,* June 17, 1987.

5. Sam Bass Warner, Jr., *Streetcar Suburbs: The Process of Growth in Boston, 1870-1900.* Second Edition. (Cambridge, Mass.: Harvard Univ. Press, 1978), pp. 11-12, 143, 32.

6. Jackson, *Crabgrass Frontier,* p. 50.

7. Ibid., pp. 188-89.

8. Ibid., p. 206.

9. Ibid., pp. 249-50.

Robert Caro and His Critics
Karen E. Markoe*

As has been the case with Boswell's life of Johnson, I suspect that future generations' notion of Robert Moses will come from Robert Caro's *The Power Broker: Robert Moses and the Fall of New York.* The book is such an extraordinary *tour de force* it is likely to eclipse whatever else is written about Moses, at least for the next generation of urban historians, city planners, and general readers. It is, warts and all, *the* record, or at least the most accessible record on Robert Moses. And who, hefting the twelve hundred plus page tome, would dare to attempt to duplicate Caro's achievement?

Because it is for now *the* record, it is important to critically assess *the* book. How did critics, both the specialists and the non-specialists, react to Caro's epic? And fourteen years later, how, in the view of urban specialists, has *The Power Broker* fared?

Virtually all the critics, Moses himself excepted, were awed by the book at its publication. Its very scope commanded respect if not reverence. But almost all, particularly the specialists, were deeply troubled as well. Perhaps historian Richard Wade expressed his reservations most succinctly: there were serious problems with methodology. Evidence was a real issue. There were too many anonymous sources and too great a reliance on interviews. Furthermore, everyone Wade spoke with who had appeared in the book in a role unfriendly to Moses believed that he or she had been misrepresented. Secondly, Wade was troubled by a lack of historical perspective. Caro attributed Moses' success to personal traits, but Wade suggested that Moses was "swimming with the tide of history."[1]

The charge of inaccuracy was one leveled by many reviewers, including some who had first-hand knowledge of one or more of the events chronicled by Caro. One of these was Dick Netzer who,

---

*This study was supported in part by a grant from the National Endowment for the Humanities.

at the time of the book's publication, was dean of the Graduate School of Public Administration at New York University. Writing in the *New Republic,* Netzer discussed his own role in Mayor Lindsay's attempt to merge New York City's transportation agencies in 1966. He derides Caro for relying "heavily on self-serving reminiscences by the two city officials who were most responsible for turning the inevitable defeat (due to Rockefeller's lack of support) into a humiliating debacle."[2]

August Heckscher, one-time Commissioner of Parks for New York City, though acknowledging his fascination with the book, also criticized Caro. "On matters with which a reader happens to be familiar," he commented, "small but annoying factual inaccuracies occur."[3]

The argument made by Richard Wade, that *The Power Broker* lacked historical perspective, was also a major theme of Jane Holtz Kay's review in *The Nation*. Writing rhetorically, Kay asked how well did Caro's New York based argument against Moses "stand up" when applied to the rest of the country, and answered:

> Look around. For if we hold to this Moses-centered view of the destruction of New York, how do we account for the same anti-urban, anti-black, carmanic, bulldozer mentality throughout the United States? Moses may have done a "better" job on New York than the other ravagers. But lacking a Moses, many other places went "his" way. *And had the author gone beyond the provincial focus of New York, his anti-hero might have appeared a rather less potent broker.*[4]

Jack Chatfield, writing in the *National Review* leveled similar charges. "I believe," Chatfield wrote, "that Caro is not careful enough about his sources. In historical research, extensive interviewing usually creates some doubt and confusion, and a writer's language reflects this."[5] And, on the matter of historical perspective, Chatfield wrote, "Caro does not consider Moses' career as part of the social and intellectual history of the American Dream. . . . Caro tries to tell the story of a life by wrenching it free from the times."[6]

The popular press, which catered to a general readership, was kinder to Caro. Peter S. Prescott, writing in *Newsday,* a publication Caro once wrote for, cheered, "Caro combines the research of a historian with the florid prose of an investigative journalist."[7] Cavilling at the extraordinary length of *The Power*

Broker, Prescott claimed Caro "takes nearly the same space to tell us about the fall of New York that Tolstoy took to tell us about war and peace."[8]

Interestingly, Philip Herrara, in reviewing *The Power Broker* for *Time,* also made reference to Tolstoy: "Can New York's master builder Robert Moses really be worth reading about in a tome longer than *War and Peace?* The astonishing answer in an age when doorstop books have become a plague, is yes—emphatically yes."[9]

Anthony Wolff, who reviewed the Caro book for *The Saturday Review,* intoned,

> The hot books these days are not soft-core porn but hard-core civics; power is the new all-American aphrodisiac. We've had the Pentagon papers, the Watergate documents, *The Best and the Brightest* and *All the President's Men.* But this book . . . is certainly the biggest and arguably the best yet, a feast to satisfy even the most prurient interest.[10]

The review that was most damning, but by critical standards said the least, was written by Robert Moses himself. It was a rebuttal of both the book and a four-part Profile that appeared in the *New Yorker* in July and August, 1974.[11] Moses' critique, just 3500 words long, was written, he said, against the advice of close friends, most of whom advised him to say nothing.[12]

Moses too criticized methodology and, in a sense, the book's lack of historical perspective. Mostly he engaged in name calling of a rather creative turn. He criticized his critics: "any ersatz bagel and lox boardwalk merchant, any down to earth commentator or barfly, any busy housewife who gets her expertise from newspapers, television, radio and telephone," and more spiritedly, "left wingers, fanatical environmentalists and seasonal Walden Ponders." At another point he referred to them as "keyhole snoopers, dirt dishers, gossips and embittered bums trying to get hunk on someone they dislike" (Moses, pp. 6, 10, 22).

Women were singled out for special rebuke. "The stink bombs of some lady critics don't suffocate us," Moses wrote. But, he added, "wild horses would not drag from me the names of these representatives of the not always fair sex." His most staunch defense, however, involved a woman:

> Among personal, nasty, false, venemous and vindictive

canards is one that I was romantically linked with Mrs. Ruth Pratt, our first Congresswoman, and that as a result my wife took sick, became alcoholic and a recluse, that I virtually abandoned her, joined some kind of foursome and took a lady who subsequently became my wife to Florida. My companion on the short Florida vacation was my daughter Jane. With respect to my family life, the author's innuendos are wholly untrue and scurrilous (Moses, pp. 16–18).

Fourteen years later I asked Caro if he still believed that the story of the affair with Ruth Pratt was true. "Of course it's true," he answered, and went on to say that Moses had many affairs, but that he had omitted them from *The Power Broker* because they were not relevant to the story.[13]

Moses cites other factual errors in Caro's work. For one thing, he wrote that he never called Mayor Fiorello LaGuardia any of the names Caro maliciously mentioned, though he conceded that he did say LaGuardia reminded him of Rigoletto. Moses also challenged what he called Caro's "exuberant Oriental fantasies" of Moses' life style. The magnificent car Caro described, Moses corrected, was his mother's old Marmon worth under a thousand dollars. Similarly, Moses wrote, the yachts were secondhand acquisitions, bought for a fraction of their worth. He added that "the magnificent meals dreamed up by Caro were cooked on sternos." These were some of "hundreds of careless errors," Moses accused Caro of though he cited only a few (Moses, pp. 21, 16, 15, 2, 3).

Moses too questioned Caro's sources, specifically Moses' dead brother who, he claimed, was a source for "dirt and misinformation." Moses noted Caro's praise of two reporters for the Scripps-Howard press; both, Moses said "were fired in disgrace after being forced to admit that they had fabricated a particularly vicious housing story."[14] Moses also charged that Caro "accepted as gospel yarns spun by Elwood M. Rabenold, once a West Side legislator." Moses recalled telling Caro that Rabenold, once charged by Moses with wheeling and dealing over the Palisades, was sent to Sing Sing for three years and disbarred in New York for stealing from an incompetent old lady whom he represented as counsel. Regarding other sources, Moses wrote, "There is no reliable evidence to be obtained from a few landowner malcontents who profited less than they expected from our improvements."

Like Richard Wade and others, Moses wondered at the underlying perspective of the author: "The biography tries to prove that I was a good boy who fell from grace, became a politician and mistreated the poor," or, elsewhere, "The author's thesis is that I was once a pilgrim who made progress, fell among charlatans, lost his inspiration and never reached the Celestial City" (Moses, pp. 14, 15, 5, 2, 11).

Moses' critique is self-revelatory at several turns, and perhaps best speaks to the veracity of Caro's portrait. Moses wrote of the "hints that my associates and I were not always ultra refined in our actions. They complain that we have not followed the Marquis of Queensberry rules." This Moses did not deny and added, "As the city folk ride into the open country, we shall, I trust, be forgiven." He then quotes Leo Durocher, archly calling him "one of our own distinguished American philosophers." Moses reminded his readers of Durocher's nice-guys-finish-last quote. At another point he writes, "I raise my stein to the builder who can remove ghettos without moving people as I hail the chef who can make omelets without breaking eggs." He does defend himself against Caro's sharpest criticism: "Ninety-eight percent of the ghetto folk we moved were given immeasurably better living places at unprecedented cost." At another juncture Moses was reminded of a quip attributed to a "departed statesman:" "Enemies—I have no enemies. I buried all those bastards long ago." And he dismissed Frank Lloyd Wright's comparison of himself to a skylark and of Moses to a blind night crawler by calling it "just a quaint bit of Celtic humor" (Moses, pp. 8, 9, 11, 4, 22).

* * *

With fifteen years having elapsed since publication of *The Power Broker*, the question should be asked, "How has the book withstood the passage of time?" Several urban specialists were, in fact, asked this question, with interesting results.

Professor Kenneth Jackson of Columbia University is a great admirer of the book. He calls *The Power Broker* "the single most important book on twentieth-century urban history ever written."[15] Jackson claims to have learned more from the Moses biography than from any other book. It is a book that he almost always assigns to students, and this was true when he was teaching in California as well as now when he is in New York.

Despite this enthusiasm, Jackson has some criticism of the book. For one thing, he shares the opinion of many that it is repetitious. He also noted that prior to Moses about one in five users of public transportation in the country was in New York City; after Moses, the figure was one in three. This hardly supports the notion that Moses was responsible for the destruction of public transportation as Caro seems to suggest. Furthermore, Jackson says, Caro ignored broad trends of history. For instance, Moses' era clearly favored the automobile, which would have prevented him from doing much for public transportation during his days of power even had he wished to. Jackson insists that Moses was a more attractive figure than Caro suggests, and that there are alternative explanations for many of the specific charges Caro levels against him, such as, the failure to build playgrounds in Harlem or building Long Island parkway bridges too low to accommodate buses.

While Kenneth Jackson almost always assigns *The Power Broker* to his students, Professor Jon Peterson, an urban historian at Queens College of the City University of New York, never does.[16] It is not that he does not find the book useful (his special interest in the history of Queens County makes the book important to him) but the extraordinary length of *The Power Broker* keeps him from assigning it in class. Peterson notes that he does not share the anti-automobile bias that underlies Caro's study.

Deborah S. Gardner, Director of the Center for the Study of Women in Business, Baruch College, of the City University of New York, has used the Caro book successfully with graduate students who respond well to the drama of it. Her own view is that subsequent readings of the work reveal Caro's one-sidedness, but she still marvels at its detail. Because of its great length, she said, "historians take pride in finishing it."[17] Gardner concluded that "the city looks very different after you read it."[18]

Richard Wade of the City University of New York Graduate Center assigns Caro's biography of Moses in his urban history seminar precisely because he disagrees with it. (For the same reason he always assigns Jane Jacobs and Lewis Mumford.)

Wade's original objections to *The Power Broker*, lack of historical perspective and questionable evidence, still trouble him. Wade had discussed the issue of evidence with Caro, and suggested that Caro might allay some of this criticism if he deposited records of his interviews in a university library, perhaps Columbia University, where scholars might assess them for themselves. Caro reportedly responded to Wade that his idea was a good one, but, in fact, did not follow through on it.[19] When I asked Caro about the conversation with Wade, he said that he did not recall it.[20]

It is Wade's opinion that Caro was interested, not in cities, but in power. Caro's biography of Lyndon Johnson also shows that, he said. Caro agreed that he is interested in power, specifically "how political power shapes our lives."[21] Caro, Wade noted, grossly overestimated Moses' power in New York City, but, interestingly, underestimated his power in the rest of the state. Wade predicted that within a decade there would be a better biography of Robert Moses, noting that already shorter studies were appearing that were at variance with Caro on key issues.[22]

Whether or not another biography of Robert Moses will hold the same fascination for readers and eclipse the impact of *The Power Broker* is a matter of speculation. It might very well be that a series of monographs will successfully challange Caro's biography of Moses on specific issues, but, for the general reader at least, Caro's account of Moses, however flawed, will remain *the* record.

NOTES

1. "The Power Broker," *The New York Times Book Review*, September 15, 1974, p. 2.
2. "The Man and the City," September 7, 1974, p. 19.
3. "The Man Who Collected Power," *The Christian Science Monitor*, September 18, 1974, p. 13.
4. "The Master Builder and His Works," September 28, 1974, p. 277. Emphasis mine.
5. "If You Seek His Monument Drive Around," December 6, 1974, p. 1420.
6. Ibid., p. 1421.

7. "Master Builder," September 16, 1974, p. 81.
8. Ibid.
9. "The Book of Moses," September 16, 1974, p. 100.
10. "Dreams of Glory, Urban Nightmare," October 19, 1974, p. 22.
11. "Annals of Politics: The Power Broker," July 22, July 29, August 12, August 19, 1974.
12. Moses Rebuttal, p. 1. Although a shorter rebuttal appeared in *The New Yorker*, I use the complete, unpublished manuscript made available to me by Professor Kenneth Jackson who received it from a Moses associate. Subsequent references are internal. (A copy of the Moses rebuttal is on deposit at the Long Island Studies Institute. Editor)
13. Conversation with Robert Caro, February 17, 1988, Columbia University.
14. Gene Gleason and Fred Cook who wrote for the New York *World-Telegram*.
15. Conversation with Kenneth Jackson, February 16, 1988, Columbia University.
16. Telephone conversation with Jon Peterson, February 12, 1988.
17. Conversation with Deborah S. Gardner, February 17, 1988, Columbia University. (Gore Vidal wrote that it took him a month to read *The Power Broker*, "Emperor of Concrete," *New York Review of Books*, October 17, 1974, p. 3.)
18. Gardner, February 17, 1988.
19. Telephone conversation with Richard Wade, February 15, 1988.
20. Caro added that he had never been approached by Columbia for his records and did not know if that is where they should go. He did not say whether, in fact, he planned to turn them over to any library. Conversation with Robert Caro, February 17, 1988.
21. Ibid. However, Caro did not agree that he was not interested in cities. The biography of Moses, Caro suggests, is a history of New York City. Caro plans to return to New York City history around 1992, when his projected three volume biography of Lyndon Johnson is completed. The new study, Caro says, will begin around 1968 and Mayor Edward Koch will figure strongly in the book.
22. Conversation with Richard Wade, February 15, 1988.

LIMITING POWER

Courtesy of Nassau County Museum Reference Library
Robert Moses, 1943

How to Rein in and Reshape Robert Moses: the Port Authority's Varied Strategies

Jameson W. Doig

In Robert Caro's version of the drama, Robert Moses—whether Robert the Visionary or Robert the Villain—has all the good parts. Through his probing intelligence, his creative aggressiveness, and several doses of plain savagery, Moses identifies what he wants to accomplish and pursues the challenge to victory. There are some missteps, certainly, mainly in his early years and near the end of his career, but in the 1940s and 1950s, particularly, Moses decides on his own goals and methods, and what Moses wants, Moses gets.[1]

A close look at the evidence indicates that Moses was less a master of his fate than Caro's rich tapestry suggests. Part of the problem is how Caro weighs his words: when Moses is Machiavellian and victorious, the story is told in exquisite detail; when Moses stumbles and falls, brevity is the soul of Caro's wit. Another part of Caro's problem is that he is too ready to embrace allegations, from friend and enemy, that Moses tended toward omniscience and omnipotence. A further search of the evidence shows that vision and dominant power were more widely shared and sometimes held in other mansions.

This essay focuses on the relationship between Moses and another important "authority structure" in the New York region, the bi-state Port of New York Authority. During the 1940s and 1950s the Port Authority confronted Moses in three important arenas; in two of these, Moses was thoroughly trounced, and in the third—contrary to Caro's view—Moses responded to rather than shaping the Port Authority's vision of a desirable world.

The first of these involved New York City's airports, which Moses wanted to control, tried to control, and saw slip from his grasp in 1946–47, as the Port Authority's leaders spun a political web which left Moses powerless and fuming. The second concerns the "largest bus terminal in the world," which the Port Authority proposed in the mid-1940s, only to face the relentless and many-sided opposition of Robert Moses and "his" City Planning Commission. The Moses opposition—quickened by his loss of the airports—delayed New York City's approval of the Port Authority plan. Yet by 1950 the Port agency had completed the gigantic Bus Terminal on Eighth Avenue in Manhattan, and Moses was once again defeated.

What you can't beat might usefully be joined in alliance, and in the 1950s Moses and the Port Authority did join forces to carry out a study of regional highways—which led to the building of the Throgs Neck Bridge, the Verrazano-Narrows span, the second deck of the George Washington Bridge, and a series of connecting highways. Caro argues that the initiative for the highway study and the main ideas for new routes were offspring of the fertile Moses brain; the evidence suggests, however, that Moses was largely responding to ideas developed within the Port Authority staff.

The second and third of these three stories will be told elsewhere.[2] In terms of the range of political strategies employed by Moses, his allies and his opponents, the story of the region's airports is the most complex of the three. And the airport story is also the most significant in terms of its results: to Moses, who lost control over a major enterprise that he coveted; to the Port Authority, which with this victory took its first important step to broaden its domain, thus becoming more than a "bridge and tunnel outfit;" and to Long Island, which has seen the two Queens airports, LaGuardia and Kennedy, grow as major air terminals and employment centers far beyond what would have been likely under the alternative Moses scheme. It is this story which will be briefly told below.

Creation and Early History of the Port Authority

While the saga of Robert Moses—who gathered government positions and political power from New York's governors and mayors through several decades—is reasonably familiar, the early years of the Port Authority are less well known and are sometimes erroneously described. In the first years of the twentieth century commercial activity in the bi-state region surrounding New York Harbor expanded rapidly, and each state sought to increase its share. However, some of the region's business and political leaders could see the advantage of a *cooperative* bi-state strategy to reduce acute congestion in the harbor and at major terminal points, and to enhance the economic vitality of the entire region in meeting challenges from other East Coast ports.[3]

An active campaign to substitute cooperation for conflict in meeting regional problems was begun in 1917, and it culminated in the creation of the Port of New York Authority—via a Compact between the states of New York and New Jersey—in April 1921. The new agency soon embarked on the specific tasks its founders had envisioned: the development of detailed plans to reduce the congestion and cost involved in handling rail and waterborne freight on both sides of the harbor, and negotiations with the railroads, whose cooperation seemed essential to success.

Despite negotiations, promises, and hopes—which continued throughout the 1920s and into 1930s—the railroads and the Port Authority staff never did make any real progress in reducing the cost of rail shipments into and across the bi-state region.[4] Meanwhile, Alfred E. Smith, New York's governor in 1919–21 and again in 1923–29, took on a pivotal role in shaping the Port Authority's future. In the mid-1920s, while he was giving new tasks to his young assistant, Robert Moses, he was also urging a reluctant Port Authority to reach beyond its initial plans and take on a new job: building bridges across the Hudson and other interstate waterways, in order to meet the growing demand for motor-vehicle travel across the region. The Port Authority soon agreed, and by 1931 the agency had completed the George Washington Bridge as well as three smaller spans.[5]

During the years 1930–32 the Authority also took control of the Holland Tunnel with its lucrative toll revenues, built a large inland freight terminal in downtown Manhattan, obtained legislative approval to construct a new vehicular tunnel under the Hudson River, and began a study of marine terminal projects in Jersey City and Hoboken. However, under the impact of the Depression the bond market collapsed in 1932, and the Authority had to seek a federal loan to enable it to go forward with the Lincoln Tunnel, which was not completed until 1937.

In the decade following the bond-market collapse, the Port

Authority's leadership took a conservative approach, concentrating on reducing costs and retiring debt rather than developing new programs. In 1942, however, the more aggressive faction of the Port Authority Board won control and selected Austin Tobin, a lawyer of immense political talent, as executive director.[6] Tobin soon organized the staff to carry out a search for new projects, and he identified the region's airports and marine terminals as prime targets for acquisition and development. During the next six years the Port Authority fought to wrest control of New York's LaGuardia and Idlewild (now Kennedy) airports, and Newark's seaport and air terminal, from their possessive city officials.[7]

Conflict Over the Airports

In reaching out for the LaGuardia and Idlewild airfields, the Port Authority found itself doing battle with New York City's mayor and with that major contender for control over airport development, Robert Moses.

Mayor Fiorello LaGuardia had spent much of 1945, his final year in office, trying to advance his own plans to improve LaGuardia Airport and to construct a vast new field at Idlewild in eastern Queens County. His City Comptroller, Joseph McGoldrick, had negotiated long-term leases with the major American airlines that—LaGuardia hoped—would solidify the airlines' commitment to the City airfields (rather than Newark) as their main base of operations in the region. LaGuardia also urged the City Council to appropriate $45 million for construction at Idlewild.

The City Council did not share the Mayor's commitment to municipal development of the airports, and deleted the appropriation in late December of 1945. In January 1946 the new mayor, William O'Dwyer, endorsed an alternative suggested by Robert Moses—turning the airports over to an independent City Airport Authority so that the City's own capital funds could be husbanded to meet urgent needs for schools, streets, and other projects. Legislation to create Airport Authority was prepared with Moses' guidance and introduced in Albany in early January.

The Port Authority responded, under Tobin's guidance, with a skillful public relations strategy. The bi-state agency argued that airport development was an immense bundle of engineering and administrative challenges which could best be undertaken by an organization with a high-quality staff and a proven track record. They also pointed out that the airports would require large amounts of funding over a period of many years before the terminals would be self-supporting, and that the Port Authority—drawing on the flow of bridge and tunnel tolls—had access to the needed funds. And they noted the advantage of developing airports on a regional basis, rather than through competition between adjacent cities. The region's major newspapers accepted these arguments and urged that the Port Authority, the only government agency which met all these standards, be given control over the air terminals.[8]

It was one thing to persuade the media that the Port Authority was the best agency to develop the region's airports. It was quite another, requiring a more variegated strategy, to meet the political challenge posed by that specific competitor for the New York City airfields, Robert Moses' City Airport Authority.

On taking office in January 1946, Mayor O'Dwyer had endorsed the Airport Authority as the best solution to the problem of developing LaGuardia and Idlewild, and he sent legislation forward for state approval. And when a citizens group proposed Port Authority operation as a better strategy, O'Dwyer responded that he was "astonished" by that proposal, for it would involve "an abject surrender of the city's planning powers" to an agency controlled by the two states. The fine hand of adviser Moses could be seen in the phrasing of O'Dwyer's rejection and in his sharp attack on the Port Authority, which he said should use its financial strength to reduce its "exorbitant" bridge and tunnel tolls rather than reaching out for the City's airfields.[9]

By early April Moses had guided the bill through both houses of the state legislature, and Governor Thomas Dewey had signed it; and on April 6, three commissioners selected by Moses and O'Dwyer were installed. The City Airport Authority now stood poised to take responsibility for the New York airfields.

To reverse the "go it alone" City policy advocated by Moses and O'Dwyer, the Port Authority would need to find allies beyond the newspaper editorial writers. Three groups were potentially of great importance: the airlines (would they view the City Airport Authority as a satisfactory way to meet their airport needs, or oppose it and favor the Port Authority?); the investment banks (would they accept airport-development bonds issued by the new Authority?); and New Jersey business and political leaders (if they endorsed the Port Authority's Newark plans, the threat that Newark Airport might be modernized rapidly and drain traffic away from the New York airfields would be far more salient). During the spring and summer of 1946 Tobin and his aides reached out to each of these three.

Even before the Airport legislation was signed, the airlines indicated that they would be wary of that "solution." The new authority flew under the banner of Commissioner Moses, who had already announced that the agency would tear up the McGoldrick-LaGuardia leases with the airlines, and that far steeper lease rates would be put into effect in order to finance the development of Idlewild and LaGuardia airports. The airlines opposed any changes in the favorable terms they had received from McGoldrick and stood ready to defend the leases in a court suit. At the same time they recognized that without massive contributions from the City treasury or some other source, the Airport Authority would be unable to develop the facilities desperately needed to accommodate rapidly expanding air traffic in the region. Capitalizing on the airlines' unease, the Port Authority contacted the airline executives and invited them to view the agency's evolving plans for Newark Airport. Airline officials expressed "great surprise and gratifications at the improvements" planned by the bi-state agency.[10]

Meanwhile, the New York Airport Authority had run into trouble. Soon after the Authority's three commissioners had been appointed, the Mayor's chief airport adviser, Robert Moses, began to intervene in their affairs. At his behest, City appropriations to be used by the Authority in developing Idlewild were reduced by $15 million, and O'Dwyer rejected an Authority request that LaGuardia Airport be turned over to that agency. Then Moses urged the Authority to issue $60 million in bonds to finance Idlewild, and to join him in denouncing the existing airline leases. But financial experts friendly to both the Port Authority and City officials advised O'Dwyer that any bonds issued by the Airport Authority probably could not be sold because of the uncertain revenue picture. Moreover, the Airport Authority chairman, Harry Guggenheim, objected to the Moses tactics, and on July 18 he resigned, advising Mayor O'Dwyer to "get the airports out of politics" by turning them over to the Port Authority.[11]

On July 30, 1946 Austin Tobin appeared before the Mayor and Commissioners in Newark and announced that the Port Authority was prepared to undertake the job of modernizing and developing Port Newark at a cost of $11 million, and that it would invest $55 million in Newark Airport, so that it could become "one of the greatest airports in the world." The Port Authority also proposed to pay $5 million in cash to Newark at the time an agreement was signed, to provide $100,000 a year in lieu of taxes, and to develop revenue sources that over a period of years would make the airport and seaport self-supporting.[12] Newark's business leaders and some of her elected officials soon endorsed the plan.

With the Airport Authority foundering, with pressure mounting to spend City capital construction funds for purposes other than airports, and with the threat of a revitalized Newark Airport now emerging clearly, it seemed inevitable that O'Dwyer would ask the Port Authority to make an offer for New York City's airfields. But Moses was still a major influence at City Hall, and Moses was vehemently opposed to letting the bi-state agency expand its domain.[13] Tobin thought an additional nudge would be desirable, in order to ensure that O'Dwyer knew the Port Authority stood ready to extend a helping hand to New York City as it had to Newark—if only O'Dwyer would ask.

That nudge was provided by Eugene Black, vice president at Chase Manhattan Bank, who had worked closely with Tobin in the late 1930s. Through a series of phone calls, Black and other Tobin allies persuaded O'Dwyer to agree, on August 2, to send a formal request to the Port Authority, asking that it "immediately" undertake studies to determine whether the Authority might be able to take responsibility for New York's airports, and thereby "relieve the city of a tremendous burden of future airport financing." The first step toward "abject surrender," as the mayor had called it six months before, had been taken.[14] The Port agency responded quickly with a study, and in December 1946 Tobin submitted a proposal to take responsibility for the City airfields.

Moses' Airport Authority was now dead, but Moses was not. Abandoning his stillborn offspring, Robert the Nimble met with O'Dwyer and urged him to keep the airports out of the hands of the Port Authority. The City could operate the airports itself, he argued, using a "bare-bones" investment strategy at Idlewild. In late February of 1947 the mayor had expressed his personal preference—to newspaper editors and to Tobin—for Port Authority operation. Two weeks later, an exasperated Tobin wrote to his Board that Moses "has swung Mayor O'Dwyer around again, full circle" to the position that the City could hold on to the airports, invest practically nothing, and "simply tell the airlines to use the facilites already installed and make the best of it."[15]

Three sharp blows broke the back of the Moses stratagem. First, Tobin took his concerns to the press, which then attacked the Moses-O'Dwyer position and endorsed the Port Authority proposal. "New York City is fumbling the ball of world airport leadership," wrote Allan Keller in a two-part feature in the *New York World-Telegram*, by trying to use a "makeshift, patch-and-ragtag program." Keller and his fellow journalists urged that New York's airports be built instead "on a stable, long-term basis by the Port Authority."[16]

Second, a close friend of Tobin's in the investment community met with O'Dwyer and emphasized the financial difficulties the City would face if it attempted to add investments in airfield facilities to its existing debt obligations. The meeting apparently shook O'Dwyer's confidence in the Moses plan.[17]

And third, Tobin agreed, although reluctantly, to modify the Port Authority's initial proposal. Earlier, when City representatives had asked if the agency could improve its offer, Tobin had resisted. The Authority had submitted the best offer it could make in view of its own financial constraints, Tobin felt; indeed, his general approach was to begin with a solid offer and oppose changes. But by March his colleagues at the Authority had convinced him that he would have to compromise if the deadlock was to be broken and the Moses strategy scuttled. In mid-March Tobin and several of his aides met with O'Dwyer's aides, concessions were made on both sides, and on March 26, 1947 the Port Authority submitted a revised proposal. On the same day the Mayor and Board of Estimate announced their agreement with the provisions of the revised plan.

So the Port Authority had won. In April 1947 the City and Authority's leaders signed a formal agreement, leasing LaGuardia and Idlewild to the Port Authority; and six months later the

Authority also sealed an agreement with Newark. Moses was left to nurse his wounded pride, and to look for other arenas where he might defeat his bi-state foe. As noted earlier, Moses found one opportunity in the Port agency's proposal to construct a massive bus terminal in Manhattan; he again fought tooth and nail, and again he lost. When the Port Authority offered an olive branch instead of a battleground a few years later, Moses grasped at it gladly, and the two giants went forward with cooperative plans to construct the Verrazano Bridge and other monuments of the late motor-vehicle age.

Final Observations

It can be argued, certainly, that the Port of New York Authority was unusual in its ability to challenge Moses. Its commissioners had close ties with governors and other political leaders, and its policies and programs were unusually insulated from his influence and retribution.[18] Its staff members were not only talented in a technical sense; they were highly effective in using their technical studies and broader strategic skills to build coalitions of support, knitting together newspaper reporters and editors, business executives, civic associations, and political leaders—spinning webs that could encircle the limbs of even the great Moses and bring him down. In his other relationships, was not Moses more likely to be dominant, more often victorious? Perhaps so; but if the Caro story of Moses is somewhat off target in this case and in the two other encounters involving the Port Authority, we should not consider Caro's descriptions of other Moses visions and "victories" as the final word.

NOTES

1. See Robert A. Caro, *The Power Broker: Robert Moses and the Fall of New York* (New York: Alfred A. Knopf, 1974).

2. In a work in progress by the author. A longer version of the present essay, which includes some of this material, is available in the Long Island Studies Institute, Hofstra University.

3. The story of the legal and political conflicts summarized here and in the next paragraph is told in detail in Erwin W. Bard, *The Port of New York Authority* (New York: Columbia University Press, 1942) chapters 1

and 2, and in Jameson W. Doig, "Empire on the Hudson," draft manuscript, Feb. 1988, chapters 2 and 3.

4. See Bard, *The Port of New York Authority*, chapters 3-6.

5. The evolution of the Port Authority into the motor age is recounted briefly in Bard; for a different interpretation, based in part on new materials, see Doig, "Empire on the Hudson," chapter 4.

6. Tobin's background and achievements prior to his selection as executive director are described in Doig, "To Claim the Seas and the Skies," in J. W. Doig and E. C. Hargrove, eds., *Leadership and Innovation* (Baltimore: Johns Hopkins University Press, 1987), pp. 129-137.

7. For more detailed discussion of the developments summarized in the section below, see Ibid., pp. 140-148, and the longer paper on deposit with the Long Island Studies Institute.

8. See for example "Area Airport Authorities Seen Needed in U.S.," *New York Herald Tribune*, Jan. 13, 1946.

9. The quoted excerpts from O'Dwyer's letter are in the *New York Times* and *Herald Tribune*, Feb. 9, 1946. On the origin and evolution of the City Airport Authority, see Herbert Kaufman, "Gotham in the Air Age," in Harold Stein, ed., *Public Administration and Policy Development: A Case Book* (New York: Harcourt, Brace, 1952), pp. 163, 165ff., and Caro, *The Power Broker*, pp. 758-763.

10. "Airlines Fear Moses Authority," *New York Post*, Feb. 6, 1946; "Air Lanes," *Newark News*, March 18, 1946; and interviews, 1984-85.

11. See Kaufman, "Gotham in the Air Age," pp. 171-175. In the previous months, Guggenheim and other members of the Airport Authority had had several meetings with Tobin, during which they explored the "tremendous demand" for airport facilities and the "regional nature" of the airport problem. (Confidential report, July 1946) For Caro's description of the difficulties of Moses and his Airport Authority in 1946 and 1947, see the single paragraph on pp. 766-767 of *The Power Broker*.

12. Port of New York Authority, *Development of Newark Airport and Seaport*, July 1946, p. 41.

13. On July 24, for example, he had denounced the idea of regional airport operation by the Port Authority; see "Airport Proposal Derided by Moses," *New York Times*, July 25, 1946.

14. See "O'Dwyer Invites Port Authority to Run City Airports," *New York Herald Tribune*, August 3, 1946; O'Dwyer's letter is reprinted in full there.

15. Port Authority Weekly Report, March 14 and 22, 1947.

16. "City Air Leadership Periled," *New York World-Telegram*, March 20, 1947, and "Airport Lag Perils 80 Million Pay Roll," Ibid., March 21, 1947.

17. Confidential document, April 18, 1947.

18. For example, the Port Authority was a bi-state agency with

strong political ties in New Jersey, largely beyond Moses' reach; also, it was beyond the control of the legislative appropriations committees in both states because tolls and rents at its own facilities generated most of its income. On these and other advantages which the Port Authority brought to its political battles, see J. W. Doig, *Metropolitan Transportation Politics and the New York Region* (New York: Columbia University Press, 1966), pp. 28ff., and M. N. Danielson and J. W. Doig, *New York: The Politics of Urban Regional Development* (Berkeley: University of California Press, 1982), pp. 196–99.

The Moses Model of Governance
David C. Perry*

The accomplishments of Robert Moses include many of the most important moments in the development of New York City in the twentieth century. To say that any other public official had literally "built" the modern city we know as New York would be to engage in hyperbole. In the case of Robert Moses, however, the description is warranted. At the beginning of his massive study of Moses, *The Power Broker*, Robert Caro takes the reader on a sweeping flight over the metropolitan New York region, pointing out that Moses built the entire modern highway system (with the exception of the East River Drive), twenty-eight state parks, 658 city parks, and directly influenced the construction of literally tens of thousands of new housing units. The "master builder," as some called him, also directed the construction of seven major bridges, the United Nations building, the New York Coliseum, and that temple of the American pastime, Shea Stadium.

Beyond these concrete accomplishments, it is apparent that Moses built more than roads, bridges, and houses; he also influenced almost every facet of urban life, from the way people traveled to the way they played, and housed themselves. Talk with almost anyone who lived in New York City during the time of Robert Moses and you will hear a vivid account of how Moses affected his or her life; he influenced, in a profound way, the physical and social relations of an entire urban population.

To hear most people tell it, Moses appeared to be bigger than life, the "powerbroker," the "master builder," the "visionary."[1] But Moses was not an urban designer who painted the landscape with broad brush strokes, fueled with political and structural omniscience. On the contrary, Moses the practitioner was a

---

*I would like to thank Jon Lines and Ellen Parker for their continuing research support, and the National Endowment for the Arts and the Triborough Bridge and Tunnel Authority for financial support. The author takes full responsibility for his conclusions.

meticulous craftsman who attacked the urban canvas in the most deliberate, comprehensive, and painstakingly detailed ways.

This meticulous attention to detail is part of the Moses legacy, a legacy as big as the city he built, and constitutes one of the features of his "model" of centralization of governmental authority. It is this model which will be examined here.[2]

Robert Moses and the Public Authority

> From the beginning it has been our conception that the function of the Authority is not merely to build and maintain certain water crossings within the city but to help solve metropolitan arterial and recreational problems.
>
> If I may be permitted a personal note, I would say it has long been a cherished ambition of mine to weave together the frayed edges of New York's metropolitan arterial tapestry. We have never lacked for plans.... What we have lacked has been unified execution.... The Triborough Bridge Authority has provided the warp on the loom, the heavier threads across which the light ones are woven ... the best use for its surplus, from both business and civic point of view, is for improvement of approaches and connections to open up new territory and improve surrounding property....
>
> Robert Moses, 1941

Here is the public Moses commemorating the fifth anniversary of the opening of the Triborough Bridge—suggesting that it is the AUTHORITY and not the bridge that might well be the important built object. Here is Moses arguing that the Authority will be the tool of urban change. But it was quite another Moses who initially used the Authority to build the Triborough Bridge.[3]

The Triborough Bridge Authority (TBA) was born not out of vision but out of fiscal expediency—a short term means for building a bridge in a financially strapped city suffering through the first stages of a long term economic depression. In fact, it was President Hoover and then President Roosevelt, fighting the national effects of the Depression, who were the early initiators of the public authority. In their attempt to devise programs which would set the nation on the road to economic recovery, Hoover, with the establishment of the Reconstruction Finance Corporation (RFC) and Roosevelt, with the panoply of programs comprising the New Deal, moved to meet the needs of unemployment and

The Moses Model of Governance

fiscal crisis in the cities with a variety of federally stimulated public works programs.

New York City was the paradigm of such economic and fiscal crisis. In 1925, the City, in the face of rising automobile usage and steady increases in population, began the process of building the Triborough Bridge. By 1927 the plans had been drawn up, and by 1929 $3,000,000 in municipal bonds were appropriated to be repaid later with tolls from the Bridge. Groundbreaking occurred on Friday, October 25, 1929—the day after "Black Thursday." After almost three years, construction of the Bridge was substantially behind schedule—the entire project mired in a political quagmire that stretched from city hall to Tammany Hall. And the Bridge was already $5,000,000 in debt, with no fiscal or political solution in sight.

James Hoey, a representative of a group of local bankers holding part of the bonds, informed Mayor John O'Brien that the situation was intolerable and future funding of the project would not be possible. In short Hoey said they were "not willing or able to finance the Triborough Bridge."[4] Hoey went on to advise the Mayor that the only possible recourse appeared to be the financial resources of the Reconstruction Finance Corporation. In fact, he said he was "confident" that the RFC would supply the money if the City legally devised the proper mechanism to financially administer and build the bridge. As a member not only of the financial community but also of the State's Emergency Public Works Commission, Hoey suggested implementation of State legislation creating a public authority for the specific purpose of completing the construction of the bridge.

For State Commissioner Hoey and his Commission Chairman, Robert Moses, the provision of public works was especially important during this period of economic emergency. The day after Hoey's communique with Mayor O'Brien, Moses wrote a memorandum to Hoey outlining an exhaustive procedure designed to ensure the successful passage and implementation of legislation creating a public authority equipped to finish the Bridge.[5]

While, at first blush, it might appear that Hoey and Moses were hatching an original strategy for financing a bankrupt public works project, the larger political and economic context suggests otherwise. Actually, they were part of a larger movement of fiscal and economic restructuring which had much of its aegis in Washington.

In the first eighteen months of his administration, Franklin Roosevelt moved fast to inaugurate a series of programs designed to attack the full range of economic conditions brought on by the Depression. In particular, he saw a vigorous public works program as a multiple instrument of recovery, providing municipalities and states with new, economically stimulating, infrastructure, citizens with jobs, and businesses with contracts.

These programs of the "New Deal" flew in the face of Roosevelt's campaign promise to end deficit financing and reduce the national debt. Only the most naive political observer could fail to notice that to offer a program of public works meant to offer an agenda of increased debt. Even though the economic benefits of public works programs were well known, the debt-ridden and tax poor conditions of the Depression era left states and localities hardly able to pitch in at a level which would guarantee an adequate use of such programs as part of the stimuli of recovery.

Roosevelt employed the Reconstruction Finance Agency and the new Public Works Administration (PWA) as new sources of funding for the beleaguered cities and states. He suggested the creation of a relatively little used, ostensibly *ad hoc*, emergency agency of government called the public authority as a mechanism by which to secure these new federal funds. The authority represented a new approach to the fiscal governance of public works inasmuch as it circumvented constitutionally prescribed debt limits imposed on the general purpose municipalities and provided the municipalities with "additional powers . . . to undertake such projects and issue bonds to finance the same: thus escaping the difficulty of gearing the legal machinery which has served municipalities of your States adequately for decades to the speed with which the Federal Government must extend credit to achieve desired results.[7] The fiscal environment, spawning the use of the public authority as a fiscal "back door" to public works construction, was indeed grim. By the middle of the decade, fifteen percent of all the municipal debt in the Unites States could not be paid at all and an estimated 3200 local governments were not able to make timely payments on the interest or the pricipal of their existing debt.[8]

In spite of such fiscal exigencies, the Supreme Court still declared the National Recovery Act unconstitutional in 1935. Although the Supreme Court upheld the right of state control over finance in the face of Roosevelt's direct attempt to establish a new direct federal-local relationship, the fiscal crisis and the continued willingness of the federal government to fund a response to the crisis could not be ignored. The public authority, once it was statutorily established by each state, represented a financially welcomed and constitutionally acceptable "back door" through which to fund public works and the jobs which came with their construction.

States created these authorities in one of two ways: by special legislative statute, or by general act of the legistature whereby local authorities were empowered to create such local authorities by election, decree or, by some other means.[9] The first option was the most popular and many states set out immediately to establish statutory, special purpose, authorities.

Spurred by federal support from the RFC and PWA, states like Pennsylvania and New York created scores of public corporations capable of selling revenue bonds to finance everything from highways to bridges and tunnels. Half of Pennsylvania's first fifty public works authorities were set up in the middle years of the 1930s and depended on the RFC and the PWA. Eleven of New York State's fifteen public authorities set up between 1933 and 1935 sold bonds to the RFC and PWA in order to inaugurate new public works programs. By the close of World War II all but seven states had used one form of legislative option or the other to set up public enterprises which could sell revenue bonds. In New York State the most dramatic example of the development and success of the public authority was the Triborough Bridge Authority, later to be renamed the Triborough Bridge and Tunnel Authority (TBTA).[10]

If the TBTA would become, in time, for Robert Moses, the "warp on the loom" of urban design in New York City, it did not start out that way. It was not the ingenious independent invention of a visionary—it was a tool forged in a climate of economic expediency—one that was also being used by many others at the federal and state level at the same time. For example, for Roosevelt, the public authority was a short-term solution to the problems of creating jobs by building needed public works in an era of economic depression. The federal government's role was that of a "banker"—no more, no less. And like any good banker, the government wanted to work with reliable risks. In Roosevelt's view the authority was the type of structure that appeared reliable. After all, the public authority, argued Roosevelt, transformed government—it was an agency which would be "clothed with the power of Government but possessed of the flexibility and initiative of a private enterprise." The authority was the best type of public agency from which the RFC or PWA could purchase bonds during such economically risky times. These bonds would secure the financing for the construction of a single revenue producing project. The public authority would maintain and operate that project until the bonds were retired, at which time the authority would go out of existence and its assets would revert to the local government in whose jurisdiction the public works project was found.[11]

The conditions leading to the establishment of the TBA could not have been more in line with the purposes of the authority as conceived of by the federal officials at the RFC. From the point of view of Moses and Hoey, not only was the city financially unable to continue building the Triborough in the wake of an economic collapse, the municipality was politically and administratively bankrupt as well. Moses believed, with some merit, that the City was not capable of completing the project and that the only way to build the bridge was to turn to the federal government. The way to engage the RFC, and later the PWA, was through an agency independent of the troubled city—a public authority.[12]

Hoey, Moses, and the rest of the New York Public Works Committee, moved to establish the TBA in the early days of the Roosevelt administration. Literally the day after Hoey notified Mayor O'Brien of the fiscal plight of the Triborough Bridge, Moses moved to plan every detail of the legislation and design of the governmental apparatus necessary to restructure the mechanisms to build the bridge. The legislation read like a model of the federal plan for such temporary authorities while, at the same time, containing a board which could ultimately make decisions that would shift the actual process of bridge-building out from under the control of city departments—including the powerful Board of Estimate.[13] The legislation specified that "said board and its corporate existence shall continue only for a period of five years and thereafter until all its liabilities have been met and its bonds paid in full."[14]

Not only did Moses write the law and design the structure of governance of the authority, he also planned every detail of its execution down to writing memos describing, in intimate and opinionated detail, the candidates for appointment to the TBA. In short, the legendary Commissioner of the Long Island Park Commission who picked the uniforms of the park attendants and chose the flowers for the parkway, was just as meticulous in overseeing every detail included in the creation of the TBA. (An undated memo from R. Moses file in September 1933 shows that he went so far as to study the relationship of the TBA to the New York Charter with regard to issues such as the printing of stationery and the design of letterheads.) For Moses, the smallest detail of practice was the stuff of power, control and ultimate success in the public realm.

In 1933, for Robert Moses ultimate success in the public realm was the completion of the Triborough Bridge. The means to this end was the public authority—the agential mechanism which freed the activity of bridge building from the inept city and gave access to the financial resources of the rejuvenated RFC under Roosevelt. The Moses of 1933 was not thinking of the public Authority in any other way—it certainly was not the warp on the loom—it was simply a means to an end—a way "to get things done."

Within a few months of the creation of the TBA, the pressure began to build the Whitestone Bridge, and to do it using the TBA. Moses and TBA head George Battle went on the record as being opposed to blending the fiscal activities of the two projects into one Authority. Battle argued that "the Authority believes it will be imprudent for it to seek to extend its interests beyond the single project for which it was created. For it to consider any other problem would be an act so far outside the scope of its authority that the Commissioners are reluctant to assume such a responsibility at this time.[15]

But Battle, the first head of the TBA, resigned within a few months due to failing health and the remaining members of the first TBA board were forced to resign with the election of the new mayor, Fiorello LaGuardia. While a new Chairman of the TBA was named in early 1934, Moses gained effective control when he was appointed Secretary and Chief Executive Officer. In this new role he assumed responsibility for every aspect of TBA operation from personnel decisions to agenda setting. His first key appointment was the selection of former Brigadier General Paul Loeser as Director of the Authority. Loeser, according to Moses, was loyal as he was aggravating—and certainly was the latter—a gruff, strict no-nonsense manager who Moses had employed previously to help him reorganize the Long Island Parks Commission.

Within days of his appointment Loeser responded to a proposal suggesting that the TBA take on the construction of the Bronx-Whitestone Bridge. Speaking for the Authority and his boss, Robert Moses, Loeser gave an answer straight from the fiscal strategy that spawned the agency, "We are not in favor of the construction of a bridge at the Point at this time ... the building of a new bridge might adversely affect the marketability of the Triborough bonds."[16]

It should be pointed out here that the resistance on the part of Moses and the members of the TBA to using the Authority to build the Bronx-Whitestone crossing should not be interpreted as resistance to the notion of the Bridge itself. On the contrary, Robert Caro points out that the Whitestone crossing had been an interest of Moses' since 1930.[17] In 1933 and 1934, the goal of Moses was to secure the funding and construction of the Triborough. The TBA was the fiscal agent and the construction manager of the Triborough—a bridge which Moses, in these economically perilous times, did not feel was a financially secure endeavor. No matter how much he wanted to build another bridge, he did not want to jeopardize the future of the Triborough. Therefore, at this time, Moses viewed the TBA as strictly a single purpose mechanism for building the Triborough. Further, Moses was in the process of shifting funding sources—from the RFC to the PWA and, along with his bonding attorneys, he was concerned that the inclusion of the Whitestone could well jeopardize the Authority's already stormy relationship with Washington.[18]

In summary, the record of Moses in the early thirties was significantly different from the public record of Moses at the end of the decade. While he may have bragged about the power of the authority in public in 1941, there is little evidence to suggest that he ever viewed the authority as a key instrument of some comprehensive plan in the early years of the decade. On the contrary, it was just another means to an end. I have written elsewhere about the transformation of the TBA from a temporary agency to the center of the public power base of infrastructure development in New York City.[19] The particular history of the TBA reflected the overall history of public authorities—an era which saw the popularization of the special purpose authority and its entrenchment as a permanent part of urban design and policy making. This general institutionalization of the public authority was a direct breach of the letter and, in most cases, the spirit of the original use of statutory public authorities. The authority was born out of fiscal and economical expendiency—in order to raise money and circumvent state constitutional debt limits in hard times. These temporary, "stop-gap" agencies were not to exist beyond the pay back period of their bonds.[20]

The TBA, under Moses leadership, became a paradigm for the transformation of the authority from its original single purpose nature to a long term, powerful, and effective agency of public works delivery. But the TBA, and later the TBTA, became more than just a multi-project agency of public works. The expansion of the formal functions of the TBA may have been similar to the expansion of the functions of authorities in other states; but the centralization of political power and policy responsibility in the TBTA was really the singular accomplishment of Robert Moses. In fact the development of what I call here the "Moses Model" of centralization of governmental functions and responsibilities in one place, one office, and ONE MAN is in many ways another lasting element of the Moses legacy.

NOTES

1. Terms used by Caro, *The Power Broker* (New York: Random House, 1974), Jameson W. Doig, "Airports, Bus Terminals, and Great Bridges: Strategies to Rein and Reshape Robert Moses," paper presented at Robert Moses conference Hofstra University, 1988, and Edward Gray, *Apostle of Progress,* unpublished script of a television movie, 1988, respectively.

2. This essay is part of a longer project on the Moses legacy of governance to be carried out as part of the research work sponsored by

the Albert A. Levin Chair of Urban Studies and Public Service at Cleveland State University. The arguments presented here are still speculative and it is hoped that through criticism and debate they will be refined.

3. See Jon J. Lines, Ellen L. Parker, and David C. Perry, *Building the Twentieth Century Public Works Machine: Robert Moses and the Public Authority,* Chicago, Ill.: The Institute of Public Works History, 1987.

4. James Hoey, letter to Mayor John P. O'Brien, March 23, 1933.

5. Robert Moses, memo to James Hoey, March 24, 1933.

6. Robert G. Smith, *Ad Hoc Governments: Special Purpose Transportation Authorities in the United States and Britian,* Beverly Hills, Calif.: SAGE Publications, 1974.

7. Franklin D. Roosevelt in 1933, as quoted in Smith.

8. See Smith, *Ad Hoc Governments.*

9. See Lines, et al.

10. Both Robert Caro, *The Power Broker,* and Lines, et al delineate this development.

11. See Lines, et al.

12. See Lines, et al, and Caro.

13. Ibid., and Delafield Hawkins, Memorandum of Advice to George Battle re: The Relation of the Civil Service Law of the State of New York to the TBA, dated Sept. 9, 1933.

14. George Battle, "Draft by Battle to Albert Goldman," attachment to letter of Robert Moses dated May 11, 1933.

16. Paul Loeser, letter dated February 17, 1934.

17. Robert Caro, *The Power Broker,* p. 341.

18. See Lines, et al, and Caro.

19. See Lines, et al.

20. Horace A. Davis, "Borrowing Machines," *National Municipal Review,* June 1935, pp. 328–44.

Rockefeller, Moses, and the Bridge That Never Was

Peter Bales

This is the story of a bridge that was never built. Though unrealized, the proposed construction of a multi-lane bridge, from the Village of Bayville in the Town of Oyster Bay across Long Island Sound to the City of Rye in Westchester, was nonetheless a political reality. The years when it was under consideration, 1965 to 1973, were years in which the machinations of both bridge supporters and opponents generated considerable attention and public interest.

Even though the bridge never came to be, the very idea that it might be built helped shape the political lives of such people as Robert Moses and Nelson Rockefeller. Fifteen years later many questions about the bridge still remain: What did it really mean to Moses? Why did Rockefeller so often shift his position on its construction? What were the real reasons behind the alliance formed by these two men? And, most important, who and what really defeated the bridge?

Robert Moses probably first envisioned a Bayville to Rye bridge in the year 1923. He had spent months that year surveying Long Island in order to map out a system of state parks that could be linked together, and to New York City, by broad parkways.[1] The parkways were eventually built as were great bridges that could link the island with the mainland. By the early sixties it had become obvious that even the Triborough, Whitestone, and Throgs Neck bridges could not handle the increasing traffic congestion. Robert Moses' solution was to build yet another bridge. And make no mistake, it was going to be his bridge. The same press release that heralded the proposed bridge project also stated that a bill was being proposed in the state legislature to amend the Public Authorities Law so that Moses' Triborough

Bridge and Tunnel Authority could operate outside the limits of New York City.²

The response of people living on the north shore of the Town of Oyster Bay and across the Sound in Rye, New York was immediate: within a couple of weeks there was a massive outcry against the proposed bridge. Civic associations formed to fight the bridge literally sprang up in both locales. Rich and important people supported these groups and made them effective instruments of lobbying and fund raising. The Gold Coast of Long Island, in particular, had many inhabitants of great wealth who were willing to donate their time and money to keep a bridge out of their backyards. Advertisements began to appear in local papers describing the bridge as a "monstrous truck route which might pass through your living room." Moses, a fighter all his life and especially cantankerous as he grew older, could not ignore the challenge. He labeled the civic associations "mushroom vigilante organizations."³

To this day, when public works are constructed in New York State one looks to the four decades of Robert Moses' tenure for precedents of operational procedures. One regular Moses policy was to go through the motions of publicly asking individuals and groups for their opinions of current proposals. But it was just that—going through the motions. The bottom line was that Moses always did what he wanted to do regardless of what opinions others expressed, for he had the power to do so. Though bound by the law, he habitually found a way to make the law work for him. Skillful manipulation of governors, mayors, judges, legislators, and voters had always cleared legal hurdles. Public hearings and unofficial studies that were not legally binding did not cause Robert Moses undue concern. When they agreed with him he extolled them. When they did not, he ignored them. Occasionally public outcry might have caused Robert Moses to delay or "lay low," but he was single-minded in his intent to see his projects through to completion. "Critics never build anything," was one of his fondest sayings, and in striving to build a Sound crossing Moses remained true to his general principles.

If Robert Moses followed Machiavellian precepts, the end similarly justified the means for the bridge opponents. The concerns of the anti-bridge activists were based singularly on self-preservation: they wanted their neighborhoods to remain undisturbed. Lofty environmental concerns were not of primary concern to the bridge foes, though they tried to make it seem that this was the case. The preservation of nature should not stop at one's property line, but the bridge opposition was quite willing to support construction so long as it was somewhere else. Oyster Bay residents in Nassau County continually tried to raise support for a span to the east, in Suffolk.[4] Bayville Mayor Duncan Sterling was so self-serving that he claimed the span belonged in Glen Cove—just a few miles to the west.[5] Local politicians on both sides of the Sound opposed the bridge because to support it, or not fight it hard enough, meant almost certain defeat at the polls. In 1967, heavily Republican Oyster Bay reelected a Democratic supervisor because his Republican rival's opposition to the bridge was perceived as "soft."[6] The same thing occurred in 1969 in a race for the town council.

To a great extent, the "Battle of the Bridge" involved the efforts of the combatants to match each other with official or quasi-official appoval of their respective positions. Studies were constantly being commissioned each of which, in turn, necessitated a counter study. Consultants hired by Moses declared that a Sound crossing was in such demand that eventually it would pay for itself through tolls.[7] Consultants hired by the bridge opponents determined that sufficient toll revenues could never be collected to make the bridge self-supporting.[8] Depending upon which expert one believed, the Bayville-Rye bridge was either feasible or folly. In reality, the consulting firms pandered to the side that hired them and each tailored their traffic projections to justify the revenue predictions they wanted to make.

Moses and his opponents both hardened their attitudes as the bridge debate continued year after year, on into the 1970s. It really was a war, motivated by obsession and hatred. Moses had gotten his Northern State Parkway and Long Island Expressway through the great estates and he was determined to do the same in the case of the bridge. In his regular *Newsday* column, Moses told what he called the north shore "booboisee" that "The person who demands complete isolation twenty miles from the city can't enjoy it very much longer, not because it is wrong to be nostalgic, but because it is futile."[9] His enemies matched him with a similar stridency. Rumors arose that accused Moses of waging a personal vendetta against the Gold Coast. His motivation: rejection from a local country club that insisted on considering Moses a Jew in spite of his conversation to the Episcopal church early in life.[10]

The main tactic of the bridge foes was to delay the start of construction for as long as possible in the belief that the passage of one inflationary year after another would drive the price "beyond the range of feasibility."[11] The effective use of hearings, fillibustering in the state legislature, and lawsuits did delay the start of construction from year to year. Delay. Delay. Delay. By 1968 no one talked about what was originally to have been a 140 million dollar bridge; the estimate had now risen to over 200 million.

Another tactic of the bridge opponents was exceptionally bold and imaginative. In late 1968, the Town of Oyster Bay cooperated with a number of private landowners to transfer 4,680 acres of wetlands to the Department of the Interior. The Interior Department for its part promised to take charge of the wetlands and preserve them in their pristine condition. The theory was that New York State would be unable to condemn the federal lands needed to build the access roads and . . . no access roads, no bridge.

The establishment of the wetlands preserve did not for an instant halt the efforts of the bridge proponents since no one knew whether the maneuver would work. The unions and construction interests felt that the move was political and that anything political could be reversed given the proper amount of lobbying.[12] Moses pressed on but he did take the threat seriously. The headline above his *Newsday* column at the time proclaimed: CONSERVATION FANATICS TRY TO BLOCK PROGRESS.[13]

Many people today credit the wetlands scheme with the ulitmate demise of the bridge. They are wrong. The wetlands remain in the hands of the Department of the Interior, but the legality of the scheme has never been tested in court. The simple truth is that the fate of the Bayville-Rye bridge was ultimately decided by one man . . . Governor Nelson A. Rockefeller.

Rockefeller's true feelings toward the proposed bridge are difficult to ascertain. Opinions of those who dealt with him on the issue differ widely. Years later, in the light of an overview, the governor's motivation became clear: Rockefeller always wanted what was best for Rockefeller. When full steam ahead was in his own best interest, that is how he proceeded. When a pro-bridge stance became a political liability, he tempered his. In the 1965–66 election year, prudence demanded that the bridge controversy be put on hold. After the election, things changed again.

New York State's finances were in deep trouble in 1967. Governor Rockefeller's years in office had been marked by massive spending that made it all but impossible for him to meet the constitutional requirement that he balance the state budget annually. Something had to be done. All transportation agencies in the state were producing large deficits except one—The Triborough Bridge and Tunnel Authority. Triborough had a 110 million dollar surplus that was growing annually. Rockefeller wanted that money and only one person stood in his way: Robert Moses.[14] In January of 1967, Rockefeller proposed a 2.5 billion dollar bond issue for the benefit of mass transportation and highway construction. Included in the bond issue was a plan to consolidate all of the New York City area commuter systems under one new agency to be called the Metropolitan Transportation Authority. By 1967 Robert Moses had only one position of power left: his chairmanship of Triborough. Under the merger plan he would lose even that. Naturally, Moses' first instinct was to fight back, and he did so with vigor. He called the bond proposal "absurd" and "grotesque," comments that received great media play.[15]

To make a long complicated soap opera short, Rockefeller used the proposed Sound crossing to win Moses' support. Theoretically, Moses still had the power to derail Governor Rockefeller's grand scheme. The Triborough Bridge and Tunnel Authority possessed over 350 million dollars worth of municipal bonds—covenants that could never be broken legally. However, on March 9, 1967, Moses had a meeting with Governor Rockefeller. Shortly thereafter Moses announced that he had completely reversed his position regarding the bond issue and the creation of the all-encompassing Metropolitan Transportation Authority. A couple of weeks later it became clear why Moses had his change of heart; Governor Rockefeller, reversing his earlier reticence, proposed that a 140 million dollar bridge be built to link the Oyster Bay-Bayville area to the Rye-Port Chester area in Westchester. Authorization for the MTA to construct such a bridge was added to the omnibus transportation bill pending in the legislature. A suit on behalf of the Triborough bondholders was never prosecuted. The Triborough bondholders' legal guardian was the Chase Manhattan Bank so the Governor was able to treat that legal hurdle as a family matter.[16]

The bond issue passed by a wide margin, though Nassau and Suffolk counties combined narrowly to vote against it. Throughout the campaign Rockefeller tried to diffuse the bridge controversy in public. He promised no money from the bond issue would be spent on the bridge and added that a long period of study and public hearings would be required before construction could commence.

Robert Moses' reign came to an end on March 1, 1968, when the Metropolitan Transportation Authority was scheduled to come into existence. After forty-four years of power, the Triborough Bridge and Tunnel Authority was gone. The head of the newly created MTA, William J. Ronan offered Moses the job of "consultant." Moses accepted and fell contritely in line behind Rockefeller and Ronan.[17] He did this because the bridge meant that much to him. Rockefeller had promised him that the bridge would be built and that when it was built Robert Moses would be the man in charge. Moses really did want it that badly. The Sound crossing was to be the grandest project of his career, his final dream, which he described poetically as "a thin passageway with a single, small, light bridge for large ships and miles of space underneath, and marinas for small ones, a crossing so low, spidery and unobtrusive as to be at most times eerie and almost invisible ... a gossamer thread over an arm of the sea."[18]

Rockefeller did fight hard for the Sound crossing in the years following his bargain with Moses, but there were critical times when he hesitated. After the victory of the bond issue in 1967, Rockefeller had all the authority he needed to order the start of work on the Bayville-Rye bridge. But he did not. He ordered another study, one that would not be completed for at least a year. Rockefeller's on-again-off-again attitude is inexplicable unless one keeps in mind that Rockefeller always did what was best for Rockefeller. In 1967, the Governor still had high hopes of getting his party's nomination for President, and his image as a wildly spending liberal was enough of a problem without the addition of a controversial bridge project. An identical scenario developed in the latter part of 1969 when the New York State Supreme Court removed the project's final legal hurdle. Public hearings could have been held and access road construction begun; neither occurred, and there was no challenge to the wetlands preserve. Once again Rockefeller ordered another time-consuming study, this time because he was running again for Governor. Whenever there was a "window"—a brief moment in time when the bridge opponents were at a loss for a legal recourse to block construction—politics caused Rockefeller to allow the opportunity to pass by. Moses waited patiently, but after the Governor's victory in 1970 it was too late.

By the late 1960s, anti-bridge sentiment had begun to spread far beyond the local communities immediately affected. There were a number of reasons for this. First, the cost of the bridge kept going up and state funds were limited. The possible need for tax increase did not sit well with legislators from all over New York State who needed to run for re-election. Second, the high cost of the Vietnam War made federal assistance uncertain. Third, and perhaps most significant, the insistent lobbying of the anti-bridge forces began to pay off. In the late 1960s, a wave of environmental concern swept the entire country, and the bridge foes rode that wave. Although the *Long Island Press* remained steadfast in its support for the Bayville-Rye bridge, the *New York Times* and *Newsday* strongly opposed it on their editorial pages.

The most crucial blow to the bridge was orchestrated by Connecticut's Senator Abraham Ribicoff when he successfully sponsored an amendment to the Federal Highway Act of 1973 that specifically barred federal funds for the Oyster Bay-Rye bridge. The House of Representatives followed suit a month later. Henceforth, if New York State wanted the bridge, it alone would have to foot the bill for the estimated 70 million dollars worth of access routes. With virtually all the state's mass transit systems producing large deficits it became clear to everyone that the bridge project would be far too expensive. Clear to everyone, that is, except Nelson Rockefeller who was not deterred by opposition which by this time, 1972, included the New York State Legislature, legislative boards from both Westchester and Nassau, the U.S. Department of the Interior, and the Congress. That Rockefeller continued calling for the bridge for nearly another year illustrates the magnitude of his commitment to the project. He really wanted the bridge, perhaps remembering a promise made to that master builder, now eighty-four, in retirement, and waiting—desperately—for the chance to procure the final jewel for his crown.

The end came swiftly and as a great surprise. When, in early 1973, both houses of the state legislature approved for the third time a bill repealing MTA authority to build the bridge, the action seemed almost routine. And it was expected that the Governor would routinely exercise his veto power. On January 20, 1973, the Governor dropped his bombshell; he ordered a halt to all planning for the Long Island Sound bridge. "People are beginning to question whether all growth is automatically good," said Rockefeller, adding that the state would henceforth concentrate on projects "which do not involve ecological problems."[19] Though Rockefeller had clearly surrendered, he refused to admit defeat. Quite the contrary, he claimed a victory; his explanation of why he had abandoned the Oyster Bay-Rye bridge attempted to raise his decision from forced surrender to an act of statemanship. "I am a lifetime environmentalist," announced the Governor. The bridge opposition, victorious, let the remark go unchallenged.

The media asked Robert Moses to comment on Rockefeller's decision. When he did, it was clear he would never surrender. "This is just a postponement," he insisted.[20] Governor Rockefeller had called personally to apprise Moses of his decision, and perhaps to apologize for being unable to keep his promise. If that was the case, Moses had no reason to feel betrayed. He had to know that Nelson Rockefeller had done his best.

Nelson Rockefeller lost the "Battle of the Bridge" because of conflicting personal priorities dictated by his position and future goals. He died in 1979 having accepted the reality that the great bridge would not be built in the forseeable future. In his last years, with his days as a public official behind him, political considerations no longer governed Rockefeller's public opinions. Unshackled, free to express his genuine feeling, he repeated several times that it "should have been built."[21] Doubtless, he was speaking what he really felt; in his years as Governor, it was during the relatively brief periods when he was not under electoral pressure that he pressed hardest for the bridge. And he did fight hard, in spite of the anger of his sister whose north shore estate would have been plowed under by the bridge, and in spite of the protests, which were the first and only time in his long career that the Governor was picketed by people wearing mink.[22]

Robert Moses died in 1981 at the age of ninety-two, bitter and angry that his great bridge remained unbuilt. But he had never given up hope that, somehow, his decades old dream would be fulfilled. Clinging to Rockefeller's promise as his only chance, he continued to sing the Governor's praises to the very end. And he never lost faith in the "Moses Approach:" more cars, roads, tunnels and bridges as the answer to America's increasing transportation needs. Only time will tell whether Moses was right.

There is no dearth of claims for credit in the defeat of the great Sound crossing. Naturally, individuals assign primary responsibility to the anti-bridge tactic they were most closely associated with. And, naturally, it is never acknowledged that motivations were mostly selfish rather than idealistic. Overall, it was a combination of pressures that defeated the bridge.

Perhaps most important, the years 1965 through 1973 were years of transition. The defeat of the bridge signaled the end of an era, an era that could be called the "Age of Moses." No longer could New York State afford to construct massive public works pandering to the automobile. Delay. Delay. Delay, indeed. Today, the cost of a bridge across Long Island Sound would be measured in the millions of dollars.

Is the Bayville-Rye bridge proposal really dead? What about a bridge somewhere in Suffolk? There can be no definitive answers. The most that can be said is that up to now, at least, there is no bridge and immediate prospects for one are bleak. Anti-bridge forces are capable of rapid mobilization to the level of their former strength; the cause remains the same and new leaders stand ready to take up the gauntlet. The pro-bridge forces are weakened by their pricipal losses: Moses and Rockefeller are both gone and neither will ever be replaced.

NOTES

1. Robert A. Caro, *The Power Broker: Robert Moses and the Fall of New York* (New York: Vintage Books, 1975), p. 10.
2. *New York Herald Tribune,* 15 February 1965.
3. *Long Island Press,* 3 February 1965.
4. Interview with Joseph Reilly, Former New York State Assemblyman, 30 November 1983.

5. *Newsday*, 7 February 1966.
6. Republican Ralph Marino lost to Democrat Michael Petito in this race. Marino's fate was sealed when it was revealed that his campaign had received a large contribution from the Lizza construction firm of Oyster Bay. Even though Marino repeatedly claimed to oppose the bridge, voters doubted his word because of his ties to the company.
7. Madigan-Hyland, Inc., New York. "Madigan-Hyland Report," 1965, p. 20.
8. Phelps, Fenn & Co., New York. "Financial Feasibility Study," 1965.
9. *Newsday*, 15 January 1966.
10. Interview with Edith Wycoff, Editor, *Locust Valley Leader*, 25 October 1983.
11. Reilly, interview.
12. Interview with Jules Kern, Caterpillar Tractor, Inc., 12 December 1983.
13. *Newsday*, 17 February 1968.
14. Caro, *The Power Broker*, pp. 1132-3.
15. Ibid., p. 1137.
16. Ibid., pp. 1132-3.
17. Ibid., p. 1141.
18. Madigan-Hyland, Inc., New York. "Madigan-Hyland Report," 1965, p. 3.
19. *New York Times*, 21 June 1973.
20. *Newsday*, 21 June 1973.
21. Reilly, interview.
22. Joseph E. Persico, *The Imperial Rockefeller: A Biography of Nelson Rockefeller* (New York: Simon and Schuster, 1982), p. 212.

QUEENS COUNTY

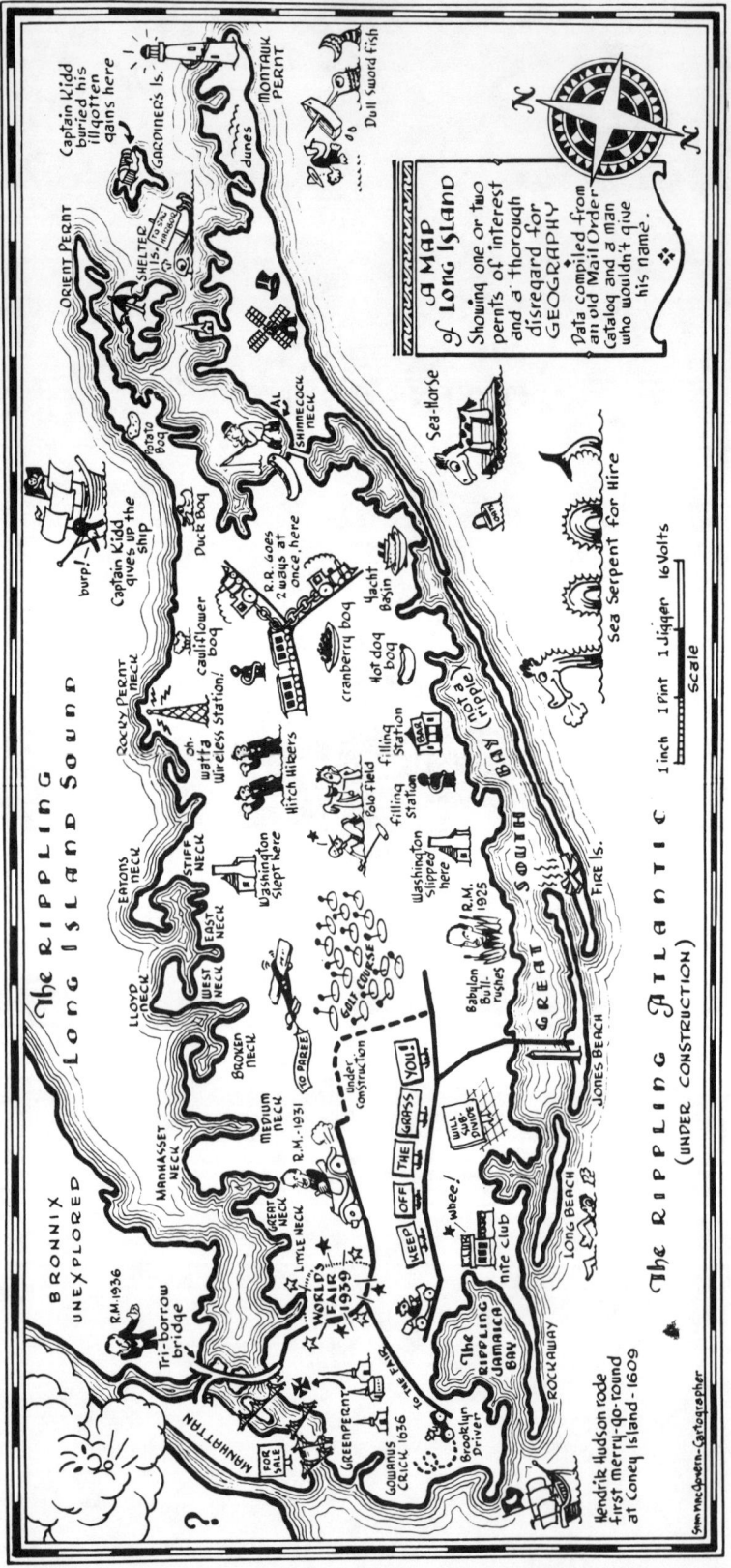

Moses' Long Island. From "All Long Island Dinner" given by the Long Island Association, April 3, 1937.

From Dump to Glory: Robert Moses and the Flushing Meadow Improvement

Helen A. Harrison

New Yorkers, like me, who grew up in Queens after World War II, think of Flushing Meadow Park as something to be grateful for, something infinitely better than what our parents told us it had replaced. To the children who skated on the roller and ice rinks of the New York City Building, swam in the Aquacade pool or prowled the neglected grounds of what had been a great world's fair, the park seemed real enough, and even functional as a recreation ground for the burgeoning neighborhoods surrounding it. But to Robert Moses, it symbolized the failure of a grand scheme that he could not admit was beyond his power to realize. For over forty years, he struggled against the odds to impose his vision on the reality of Flushing Meadow.

It should be remembered that, in conceiving a park on the tract of land extending south from Flushing Bay along the banks of the Flushing River, Moses was not envisioning a landscaping project or the provision of superficial amenities. No mere beautification effort would suffice. By the 1920s, this terrain, originally a marshy estuary created as the bay's waters receded after the last Ice Age, had become the infamous "valley of ashes" immortalized in F. Scott Fitzgerald's novel, *The Great Gatsby:*

> ... a fantastic farm where ashes grow like wheat into ridges and hills and grotesque gardens; where ashes take the form of houses and chimneys and rising smoke and, finally, with a transcendent effort, of ash-grey men who move dimly and already crumbling through the powdery air.... The valley of ashes is bounded on one side by a small foul river, and, when the drawbridge is up to let barges through, the passengers on waiting trains can stare at the dismal scene for as long as half an hour.[1]

The deliciously evocative image of a vast moonscape created

Courtesy of The Queens Museum

Corona Dumps, January 1933

by the dumping of millions of cubic yards of smoldering furnace waste larded with tons of household garbage made a compelling literary symbol, but one that required no leap of the imagination. The ghastly dump—the creation, not of a writer's mind but of the Brooklyn Ash Removal Company—was a desecration that shamed the surrounding communities and angered Moses, who never lost sight of the fact that underneath it lay "a beautiful tidal basin, where farmers and townspeople harvested crops of salt hay, fish, crabs, clams, oysters and wild water fowl."[2]

In planning his parkway system for Long Island, Moses imagined the dump as an extensive right-of-way that could be reclaimed as part of the highway construction program. With an area of over 1,200 acres, half again the size of Central Park (840 acres), Flushing Meadow offered an even greater prospect than Olmsted and Vaux had faced. Moreover, the land was at the geographical hub of the city, and promised to be at the center of its population before long. It was clear at the outset, however, that neither the city nor the state was willing to spend the vast sums required to transform the dump. Especially during the Great Depression, as Moses ruefully noted, "this dream seemed too big for the vision and means of the city in the face of so many other urgent enterprises."[3]

Yet it was the city's determination to overcome the Depression's economic and social ills that enabled Moses to set his plan in motion. In 1933-34, New York businessmen watched with a combination of curiosity and envy as Chicago drew international attention with its "Century of Progress" exposition, which remarkably returned a modest profit to the city and was reported to have injected some $770 million into the local economy.[4] A delegation of commercial and financial interests sent to Chicago in the summer of 1935 came back with an enthusiastic report, and estimated that New York could benefit from a similar enterprise to the tune of at least a billion dollars.

The idea of holding a world's fair in New York had crystalized the previous spring in the mind of a Queens resident, Joseph Shadgen, an engineer born in Luxembourg and then living in Elmhurst. Foreshadowing the decisive influence the immigrant community would have on the area's development, his professional acumen suggested that nearby Flushing Meadow offered the ideal combination of convenient location and a large area of unoccupied, virtually derelict, land. Shadgen promoted his concept to George McAneny, President of Title Guarantee & Trust and a member of the business group searching for ways out of New York's Depression doldrums, who took it to Moses for an opinion on its feasibility. As Moses later wrote, "I told Mr. McAneny that I would stop at nothing to help him . . . if the fair were actually to be in Flushing Meadow, and if from the beginning the project was planned so as to insure a great park in the geographical and population center of the city."[5]

Although he was one of the few officals involved in its planning to give credit to Shadgen for the idea of bringing the fair to Flushing, Moses was, in effect, simply bolstering the argument he had been making since the inception of the Grand Central Parkway extension, which bisected the dump on its way to the Triborough Bridge, and which he had hoped would provide funds for at least landscaping of the area. Beyond capitalizing on the construction funds generated by the fair's bond issue, along with federal, state and city financing, he negotiated with the Fair Corporation for a $4 million cut of the anticipated profits, with which he planned to convert the grounds into no mere recreation ground, but rather nothing less than "the Versailles of America."[6]

The initial prospects for such an ambitious undertaking were not encouraging. Grover Whalen, President and chief spokesman of the Fair Corporation, described the site on the day of groundbreaking, June 29, 1936, in unflattering terms:

> Everywhere was the odor of buried and smoldering rubbish. As we plowed through the rubble after leaving the cars at the road's edge ... one of my friends turned and said, "Grover, I hope you know what you're doing. Doesn't look to me as if anything can ever be done with this dump!"[7]

Whalen characterized his fellow fair promoters as "a group who believed that it paid to advertise," and this held equally true for Moses. Three months after the groundbreaking, when 450 men working 24–hour shifts had moved over two million cubic yards of debris in the initial phase of site preparation, his office issued the first in a series of bulletins known as the *Flushing Meadow Improvement*. In it, he publicly chronicled the progress of Flushing Meadow as it was transformed, in his words, "from dump to glory."[8]

Courtesy of The Queens Museum

From Dump to Glory   95

   As a propaganda vehicle, the publication, although ostensibly devoted to describing the development of the site for the fair, was relentless in its focus on the permanent, enduring aspects of the project. Its opening article outlined, not the magnificent exposition scheduled to open in a scant two and a half years, but the magnificent park that would immediately replace it. To Moses, who publicly labeled it "iridescent froth,"[9] the fair seemed to be little more than an inconvenient delay in the implementation of his park scheme. This scheme involved the provision of a wide variety of amenities, including athletic fields, playgrounds, swimming and wading pools, a pitch-putt golf course, a model yacht basin, and an outdoor amphitheater. Designed as the "active

Courtesy of The Queens Museum

Main Section of the planned park

recreation center," this would encompass the 373-acre area where the fair's main exhibits would be grouped. Interestingly, the city and state exhibit buildings would be constructed as permanent recreation structures that would be converted for temporary use as fair pavilions, rather than the other way round which might have been the case had Moses not been truly planning a park rather than a fairground. Beyond the main section, in areas largely devoted to "passive recreation," a host of other facilities were planned, all described and illustrated in thrilling detail: a marina on Flushing Bay, an arboretum bordering one of the two artificial lakes, bridle paths, and parking fields, and all ornamented with walks, drives, malls, reflecting pools, and extensive plantings.

The purpose of such precise and thorough recitation was clearly to convince both the public at large and the officials responsible for approving and financing these improvements that the plan was not only feasible, but that it was in fact a foregone conclusion. The bulletin itself was not designed for wide dissemination, but was evidently intended to shape popular opinion via the news media which would distill from it material with which to fill reports on the fair's progress. Moses wanted the public to be aware that the fair was a means to a greater end, not an end in itself. His publication thus became more than a simple house organ aimed at keeping insiders apprised of the project's step-by-step progress. With a lively text and ample pictures, he telescoped the past, present and future of Flushing Meadow into a saga of benevolent civic enterprise repairing the ravages of carelessness, replacing ashes with beauty for the common benefit.

To insure that the fair would provide a suitable foundation for his redevelopment scheme, Moses could count on the influence of Gilmore Clarke, his trusted consultant landscape architect, who sat on the fair's seven-member Board of Design. As Clarke later recalled, it was probably George McAneny who had recommended him for the crucial position, and McAneny was Moses' conduit to the Fair Corporation. Though remaining in the background, Moses was nevertheless able to promote his interest in the fair's long-term potential via Clarke's standing on the design board. In Clarke's view, Moses "didn't have much to do with that '39 World's Fair. Of course, if you asked Bob, talked to him about it, you'd think that he had everything to do with it."

Fundamentally, Moses did have everything to do with the fair, in that his vision determined its physical form, for it was Clarke who conceived the highly formalized, Beaux Arts radial plan that was adopted for the main exhibit area. "He was glad to have me there [on the design board]" Clarke recalled, "because he was pretty sure he'd get something rational.... I was conscious of the fact that this was going to be a public park, so my design was prepared with that in mind for the future...."[10]

Among the competing ideas described in the board's records and by other architects I have interviewed, Clarke's design was the most traditional.[11] "That didn't please some of the younger architects who worked in the offices related to the board," Clarke admitted. "They wanted something higgledy-piggledy, with no center of interest that would be focused." But it was the board's desire to express a unifying theme for the fair that enabled Clarke to prevail. "The plan that I fashioned gave them a central point to put something," he said. "It gave a focus, and the plan lent itself to a reasonable design for a park afterwards. This park didn't lend itself so well to informality because it was absolutely flat."

To compensate for the site's lack of topographical character, Moses provided visual interest through landscaping and planting designed to outlive the fair. Not so visible, but equally crucial to the park's viability, were the massive engineering improvements required to stabilize the area and provide it with road and rail access for what Moses envisioned as "patronage from the greater city as a whole ... from other boroughs and from regions outside the city limits."[12] These projects included the construction of a tide gate and dam, provision of two sewage treatment plants, a railroad drawbridge, access roads, pedestrian bridges, rapid transit lines, improvements to adjacent streets and highways, and some of the largest storm sewers ever constructed. Details were faithfully recorded in the *Flushing Meadow Improvement*, along with a series of articles titled "After the Fair," in which the permanent benefits of past fairs, from the 1853 Crystal Palace, New York's first international exposition, to the 1876 Centennial Exposition in Philadelphia and the 1893 World's Columbian Exposition in Chicago, were described in glowing terms.

Unlike the *World's Fair Bulletin*, the official publication of the

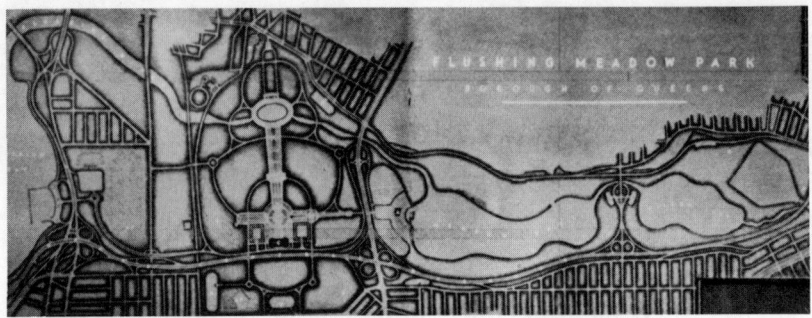

Courtesy of The Queens Museum

After the Fair

Fair Corporation, Moses' brochures treated the fair as secondary to the grand scheme—his scheme—for Flushing Meadow. But ironically, while acknowledging that the fair was the instrument of the plan's realization, he could not foresee that it would ultimately become the park's undoing. Counting on the $4 million from fair profits to bankroll the final phase of park construction, he was bitterly disappointed when "this proved to be wooden money because there was a deficit instead of a balance, and our source of future development funds simply evaporated."[13] Considering the past successes of post-fair parks in Chicago and Philadelphia, publicized in his own brochures, this humiliation was all the harder to swallow.

Even today, as succeeding administrations continue to struggle with the seemingly intractable problems of Flushing Meadow Park, we must marvel at Moses' persistence, a drive that led him to renounce so much of his power to accept the presidency of the second fair on the site. No more effective than its predecessor, the 1964–65 fair left its own legacy of debt and disillusionment, along with a still unfinished park. On the occasion of its somewhat premature public dedication in 1967, he reminisced about the odyssey "from dump to glory," admitting that the journey was not yet ended when he wrote that "every step . . . follows an ultimate plan which is realizable in the not distant future."[14]

As surviving drawings show, Moses was still committed to a vision of the park largely formed in 1936: a manicured landscape of rigidly controlled zones and orderly recreation. By trying to impose such a high degree of formality, with its attendant maintenance and policing requirements, on such a large, accessible, and unstable site, Moses was saddling the city with a fiscal and administrative burden beyond its resources. The dilapidated state of many of the facilities in the so-called "active recreation center," and the modifications that have weakened and in some areas obliterated the original concept, attest to the fact that, in this section of America at least, the glories of Versailles remain elusive, perhaps unattainable.

NOTES

1. F. Scott Fitzgerald, *The Great Gatsby* (New York: Charles Scribner's Sons, 1925 [1953]), pp. 25–26. The dump was opened around the turn of the century. Although I have not been able to determine the exact date of its inception, a *Report on the Collection and Disposal of Solid Wastes in the City of New York* (1921), states that, "In Brooklyn, the disposal of ashes, street sweepings and rubbish is done by contract and this has been the practice for over eighteen years." According to the report, the Brooklyn Ash Removal Company's property at Corona, L. I., was then "where all materials placed upon [the company's garbage] scows and [railroad] cars are taken and used for filling low land." (p. 6). I am grateful to Devra L. Zetlin of the Department of Records and Information Services, Municipal Reference and Research Center, for bringing this document to my attention.

2. Robert Moses, "The Saga of Flushing Meadow," originally written in 1966 and partially reprinted in the souvenir brochure for the dedication ceremonies, Flushing Meadows-Corona Park, June 3, 1967, pp. 7–24 (p. 7). Cf. Robert Moses, *Public Works: A Dangerous Trade* (New York: McGraw-Hill, 1970), pp. 536–543.

3. Moses, "Saga," p. 8.

4. Grover Whalen, *Mr. New York* (New York: G. P. Putnam's Sons, 1955), p. 174.

5. Moses, "Saga," pp. 8–9. In fact, Moses had set his plan in motion more than a year and a half earlier. On 2 February 1934, *The New York Times* reported the Board of Estimate was about to consider a proposal to turn the Corona Dump into a recreation area ("Ash Dumps May Be Park," p. 19, col. 5). When the fair plans were officially announced in September 1935, the *Times* noted that: "The area had been picked by the city for park and municipal golf purposes and development already has been under way. It is known as the proposed Flushing Meadow Park." ("Site is Selected on Flushing Bay," 23 September 1935, p. 14, col. 1). This report somewhat undermines Moses' retrospective contention that the park could not have happened without the Fair, but the extent of

"development" is not mentioned. It may be conjectured that the plans were less concrete than theoretical in 1934.

6. *The Flushing Meadow Improvement:* Official Organ of the Public Officials in charge of Basic Improvements at Flushing Meadow Park, compiled under the direction of Robert Moses, Park Commissioner, vol. 1, no. 1 (October 1936), p. 1. (Published intermittently between October 1936 and 15 May 1939.)

7. Whalen, *Mr. New York*, p. 198.

8. *Flushing Meadow Improvement*, October 1936, p. 1.

9. Robert Moses, "After the Fair, Flushing Meadow Park," New York *Herald Tribune* World's Fair Supplement, 30 April 1939, p. 54.

10. All information about Clarke's involvement in the project, and direct quotes of him, are taken from an audiotaped interview with the author, 9 June 1980.

11. Specifically, material contained in the Board of Design records in the 1939/40 New York World's Fair Collection, Manuscripts and Archives Division, New York Public Library, and audiotaped interviews by the author with architects Ian Woodner-Silverman and Wallace Harrison. Woodner-Silverman described a serpentine plan, while Harrison recalled a proposal for right-angle avenues intersecting at T-junctions.

12. *Flushing Meadow Improvement*, December 1936, p. 3.

13. Moses, "Saga," p. 11.

14. Moses, "Saga," p. 24.

I would like to acknowledge the cooperation of The Queens Museum, whose World's Fair Collection contains an incomplete set of *The Flushing Meadow Improvement* (gift of Frank Pokorney), and the Map Room of the New York City Department of Parks' Olmsted Center in Flushing Meadow Park, where Joseph Coticcio put many of his records at my disposal.

Robert Moses and the New Deal in Queens
Jeffrey A. Kroessler

For America's cities the Great Depression brought an unprecedented level of unemployment and the nearly total collapse of such cornerstones of urban prosperity as the real estate market. While not exclusively an urban problem, unemployment was certainly more visible in the cities, and by their numbers and the nature of their demands the jobless soon overwhelmed all sources of private charity. In 1932 alone, financial institutions foreclosed on a quarter of a million properties; by the time Franklin Delano Roosevelt took office in March 1933, the foreclosure rate in the nation was up to a thousand a day.[1]

With Roosevelt came the "New Deal," his administration's dynamic program of public works, relief, and reform. The dimensions of the urban crisis caused by the great depression are most clearly seen on the local level, and, within New York City, the Borough of Queens offers an instructive case study. The largest of the five boroughs in area but surpassing only Staten Island in population, Queens prospered during the boom years of the 1920s. New rapid transit lines carried residents between jobs in Manhattan offices or Long Island City factories and homes in new suburban developments arising on open stretches of land. Almost overnight, following the stock market crash, the mood of optimistic boosterism felt earlier in the borough yielded to cries for governmental action to ease the crisis.

As the nation's greatest metropolis, New York City was unique in both the magnitude of its problems and in the scope of its solutions. The city was fortunate to have an activist mayor in Fiorello H. LaGuardia and an invaluable asset in Parks Commissioner Robert Moses, who actually increased his power during the New Deal despite Franklin Roosevelt's animosity. One example of this increase came about in January 1935 when the

Queens Chamber of Commerce demanded that Moses remain on the Triborough Bridge Authority and keep his position as Parks Commissioner as well.[2]

LaGuardia and Moses understood better than anyone the implications of the New Deal for cities, and they were adept at using those innovative programs to New York's advantage. Under their creative leadership the city received millions of dollars in aid for dozens of construction projects, large and small. At the groundbreaking ceremony for the Queens-Midtown Tunnel on October 2, 1936, President Roosevelt remarked, "Every now and then I would hear that your Mayor had slipped off to Washington, and each time I say to myself, 'There goes another $5,000,000 or $10,000,000.' But I was glad to help, because everything that was initiated was a useful project."[3]

In Queens alone, between 1933 and 1940, federal dollars went into the Triborough and Whitestone Bridges, the Queens-Midtown Tunnel, the Belt Parkway, a new Queens Borough Hall and Court House, the Queensbridge and South Jamaica housing projects, LaGuardia Airport, Astoria Park and Pool, Juniper Valley Park, the Rockaway Beach Improvement, Riis Park and the Marine Parkway Bridge, and, finally, the 1939 World's Fair, the "World of Tomorrow." Robert Moses was responsible for almost all of these projects.

Public works transformed the Queens landscape from one end to the other during the New Deal, and Robert Moses played a central role in that transformation, from the Triborough Bridge to the Rockaway Improvement, a redevelopment of the beach and boardwalk. It is important to remember, however, that all of the projects with which Moses is closely identified depended on cooperation between several governmental agencies and, above all, the political will to commit the necessary resources toward their realization.

The key to the remarkable transformation of Queens during the 1930s is the way each project was initiated in relationship to others in the city. That Robert Moses was simultaneously New York City Parks Commissioner and Chairman of the Triborough Bridge Authority made such linkage not only possible, but essential. The Triborough Bridge, for example, not only linked Manhattan, the Bronx, and Queens, but also featured a network of fourteen miles of approach roads stretching from the East River

Drive to the Kew Gardens Interchange, also known as "the Pretzel," the point where the Interboro Parkway, Grand Central Parkway, Queens Boulevard, and Union Turnpike meet.

Along the way Moses appropriated a significant part of the Corona Dumps not only for the parkway, but also for new parks and playgrounds. Astoria Pool was built in the shadow of the new span, and on Randall's Island Moses planned for a new municipal stadium. On the Bronx side the approaches linked up with the Westchester parkways, and an additional highway signified by a dotted line on the map closely follows the route of what is now the Major Deegan Parkway.[4]

It is paramount to keep in mind that Moses' rise to power came in the context of the New Deal. True, he did leave his mark on Long Island during the 1920s, and the parks and parkways in Nassau and Suffolk testify to his achievements, but power, the kind of arrogant power which Robert Caro describes and which distinguishes Moses the Dreamer from Moses the Power Broker, came during the 1930s when the federal government made an unprecedented commitment to public works in response to massive unemployment.

The New Deal made possible projects like the Triborough Bridge and the Queens-Midtown Tunnel (one of the few public works projects in Queens with which Moses was not associated), but the ideas did not originate then. A 38th Street Tunnel had been proposed as early as 1921, when traffic on the Queensboro Bridge was already intolerable. Plans for the Triborough Bridge were drawn up in 1927 and funding was approved by the Board of Estimate in 1929, in which year Mayor James J. Walker presided at the ground breaking. Unable to continue financing the bridge in the face of demands by its citizens for relief during the early years of the depression, the city abandoned all work on the project. Only the massive infusion of $44 million in federal grants and loans in September 1933, and the reorganization of the Triborough Bridge Authority in 1934, with Robert Moses as one of the new members, made possible the completion of the bridge. Of the $44 million, only $9 million came as an outright grant from the Public Works Authority, the remaining $35 million coming in the form of loans to the Triborough Bridge Authority.[5]

One dimension of the story of the Triborough Bridge highlighted by Robert Caro in *The Power Broker* has to do with the

Manhattan terminus of the span located at 125th St. Caro contends that it was pressure from Hearst interests which dictated the location of the entrance in Harlem. While professing a battle against interests, Moses is said to have actually caved in to those interests. In fact, the earliest plans for the bridge, drawn up long before Moses joined the Authority, called for the terminus to be at this point.[6]

While it was impossible for Moses to change the plans after he became a member of the TBA, he did make the most of the inefficient route by including fourteen miles of approach roads in the three boroughs, thereby transforming an essentially local project necessarily tied to local interests into "a modern metropolitan traffic artery" designed to knit the region together.

Furthermore, Moses "borrowed" the distinguished engineer O. H. Ammann from the Port of New York Authority. Ammann immediately redesigned the bridge, rejecting existing plans for a two-level span with sixteen narrow lanes in favor of a single deck with eight wide lanes. In the process, the costly granite which was intended to cover the towers was eliminated, thus saving millions of dollars and enhancing the beauty of the steel span.[7]

True, Moses' part in the closing of the 92nd St.-Astoria Ferry and the removal of hospitals from Randall's Island exemplifies his penchant for disregarding legal, bureaucratic, or ethical hurdles in his drive to get things done, and in that sense Caro's criticism of Moses is justified.[8] Still, the Triborough Bridge was the first of Moses' accomplishments during the New Deal, and his insistence that landscaping, parks and playgrounds, and public access be essential components of this project set the pattern for later projects in Queens.

Jones Beach was probably the most successful of Robert Moses' undertakings, and the expansion of public works during the New Deal gave him an opportunity to recreate that success at Rockaway. His goal was to return a clean and uncluttered beach to the public by removing the private interests that had crowded the beach with concession stands, hotels, and bungalows. (He had similar plans for Coney Island calling for the elimination of the rides and amusements.) According to Moses, "The Rockaway Improvement may not be a model to be followed in the development of unspoiled beaches. I believe, however, that it will be a guide to those who seek to reclaim beaches which man has spoiled, and to restore them at least measurably for the purposes to which they were intended by nature."[9]

The Rockaway Improvement was financed by linking it to reconstruction of the Cross Bay Boulevard and construction of the new Marine Parkway (now Gil Hodges) Bridge to Riis Park. The master plan called for connecting Rockaway with the Belt Parkway then under construction and the future development of Jamaica Bay for recreational pursuits. At a time when plans for a deep water port in Jamaica Bay were still seriously proposed in some circles, and when indeed the proposed port appeared on the offical city maps, Robert Moses saw Jamaica Bay preserved "in its natural state for recreational and residential purposes.[10]

In July 1938, Moses issued a report through the Department of Parks titled "The Future of Jamaica Bay," a booklet which embodied a set of Moses' values: public access to recreational facilities in a clean environment, removal of private interests, and a vision of what the metropolis could, and, in his eyes, should be. What set off the publication was a proposal floated by the city sanitation commissioner to establish a dump in the middle of the Bay; a "civic nightmare," Moses called it. Yet with the closing of the Corona Dumps and the redevelopment of Flushing Meadows as the site of the World's Fair, New York did in truth need a new site for its refuse.

The ash dump and massive incinerator suggested for Jamaica Bay was actually the last gasp of an early twentieth-century plan to construct in the Bay a deep water port larger than Liverpool, Hamburg, and Rotterdam combined. The ash and garbage dumps, as well as material dredged from the bottom to create the channels, would provide the landfill for two great islands in the center of the Bay. In its original conception, the Jamaica Bay Port would have been connected to the mainland via a railroad tunnel under the Narrows.[11]

Moses called on the city to finally decide between the two seemingly irreconcilable visions of the Bay: an industrial port (an idea which in fact had been dead since the mid-1920s when the Port Authority decided to redevelop Newark Bay,) or, in Moses' words, "a place within the limits of the city where the strain of our city life can be relieved, where the nerves of tired workers may be soothed, where the old may rest and the young can play." This was classic Moses rhetoric, espousing his version of civic virtue.

Concluding his reasoned ("What we need in this context is a little common sense") with an emotional appeal, he argued:

> Jamaica Bay faces today the blight of bad planning, polluted water, and garbage dumping. Are we to have here another waterfront slum, depriving millions of future inhabitants of Brooklyn and Queens of the advantages of boating, fishing, and swimming in safe inland waters? Must we continue the construction of expensive, artificial swimming pools in this region, where the waters of Jamaica Bay, protected from pollution, can meet the problem as nature intended it to be met?[12]

Of course, one of the "expensive, artificial swimming pools" was his own Astoria Pool, built in conjunction with the Triborough Bridge in 1937 and site of the Olympic trials that year. Moses was a master at setting up a straw man—"private interests," "blight," "expensive," "artificial,"—to advance his proposals.

Neither the Rockaway Improvement nor "The Future of Jamaica Bay" was an independent effort; redevelopment of Riis Park, the new Marine parkway Bridge, the widening of Cross Bay Boulevard, the Belt Parkway, and Canarisie Beach Park were all initiated simultaneously, were intended to fit together, with bridges and highways feeding into recreational facilities, and together represented a strong sense of the future of the city.[13] In retrospect, it seems appropriate to give Moses credit for saving Jamaica Bay from the blight of garbage dumps and industrial development, especially since it is today part of the Gateway National Park and a thriving wildlife refuge, and the water is not nearly so polluted as it was in the 1930s. While it is indeed true that portions of Moses' vision have been realized, and the Bay has been reserved for residential and recreational uses, there is nonetheless a large, nearly full garbage dump along the shore near the Brooklyn-Queens border. Moses may have successfully opposed the construction of an immense ash dump and incinerator in the heart of the Bay, but other interests and concerns compromised his vision.[14]

A third set of projects in eastern Queens focused on the World's Fair. As far as Moses was concerned, the primary virtue of the "World of Tomorrow" was the reclamation of the dumps so vividly described by F. Scott Fitzgerald in *The Great Gatsby* and their transformation after the Fair into a great park. Components of this vision included the Cross Island Parkway (an essential link in the Belt System), the Bronx-Whitestone Bridge (which required only twenty-three months between ground breaking and opening and was acknowledged as the most graceful suspension bridge ever built, at least until design flaws forced the installation of steel stabilizers which eliminated the pedestrian walkways), and additional approach highways and bridges to Flushing Meadows, not to mention the new municipal airport at North Beach (renamed LaGuardia Airport shortly after its opening in 1939). Since the Cross Island Parkway was only for passenger cars, a new mixed-use artery, Francis Lewis Boulevard, was built from the Whitestone Bridge through Cunningham Park, which was also slated for improvement.[15]

The New Deal landscape finds its most complete expression in the Borough of Queens, from neighborhood health care facilities to new parks and playgrounds, from insuring mortgages to building public housing on schedule and under budget. Among the most permanent of these accomplishments were the public works. Far from "make work" projects, public works thrust Queens into the automobile age. Highways and bridges were planned as vital links in a modern, metropolitan system, rather than essential local efforts addressing local concerns. The Regional Plan Association may have envisioned such arteries in the 1920s, but only the energy, commitment, and political will of the New Deal made their realization possible. Those circumstances also gave Robert Moses the opportunity to exercise power on a grand scale. The result was nothing less than the transformation of Queens from a nineteenth to a twentieth-century urban landscape.

NOTES

1. Nathaniel S. Keith, *Politics and the Housing Crisis Since 1930* (New York: Universe Books, 1973), p. 13–19.

2. *Queensborough (QB)*, Queens Chamber of Commerce, January 1935; p. 10–11.

3. *QB*, October 1936; p. 212.

4. Moses, *The Triborough Bridge: A Modern Metropolitan Traffic Artery* (New York: The Triborough Bridge Authority, 1936); see also photographs in the Triborough Bridge and Tunnel Authority files, and in

the Parks Photo Archive, Parks Historian's Office.

5. Moses, *The Triborough Bridge: A Modern Metropolitan Traffic Artery*, 1936.

6. *Long Island Press*, July 26, 1937.

7. Moses, *The Triborough Bridge: A Modern Metropolitan Traffic Artery*, 1936.

8. Robert Caro, *The Power Broker: Robert Moses and the Fall of New York* (New York: Vintage Books, 1975), pp. 448–51.

9. NYC Department of Parks, "The Rockaway Improvement," 1939; for Moses' plans for Coney Island, see NYC Department of Parks, "The Improvement of Coney Island, Rockaway and South Beaches," 1937; and NYC Department of Parks, "The Improvement of Coney Island," 1939.

10. NYC Department of Parks, "The Future of Jamaica Bay," 1938.

11. See N. B. Killmer, "The Authorized Freight and Passenger Tunnel under the Narrows between Brooklyn and Staten Island; Its Conception, Object and Benefits to be Derived; Its necessity shown not only for the success of the Jamaica Bay Development but for the Future Growth and Prosperity of the Greater City of New York," New York: Jamaica Bay Improvement Association, 1925; see also maps in the Long Island Division of the Queensborough Public Library, especially "Plan for Development of Jamaica Bay, submitted by the Dept. of Docks & Ferries," and "Map of Jamaica Bay," Feb. 10, 1930.

12. NYC Department of Parks, "The Future of Jamaica Bay," 1938.

13. "The Future of Jamaica;" NYC Department of Parks, "The Rockaway Improvement," 1939; "Circumferential Parkway" (New York: The Moore Press, Inc., 1938); Marine Parkway Authority, "The Marine Parkway," 1937; see also photos of the redevelopment of Rockaway Beach in the Long Island Division of the Queensborough Public Library, and the Parks Photo Archive, Park Historian's Office.

14. Robert Caro mentions neither "The Future of Jamaica Bay" nor the controversy over the garbage dump and incinerator.

15. Moses, "From Dump To Glory," *The Saturday Evening Post*, January 15, 1938; "The Bronx-Whitestone Bridge," New York: Triborough Bridge Authority, 1939; "Completion of Francis Lewis Boulevard, Queens, Mixed Traffic Approach to the Bronx-Whitestone Bridge," New York: Triborough Bridge Authority, 1940; "The Circumferential Parkway," 1938; see also photos in the TBTA files and the Parks Photo Archive, Park Historian's Office.

The Man Who Changed the Map of Queens: A Personal View

David Oats

As a twelve-year-old kid growing up in the James A. Bland Housing Development in Flushing, Queens, my backyard was Flushing Meadows Park. There was a small asphalt playground in the project complex, but the real days of summer play were spent at the big park just a few blocks away. You could swim in the Aquacade during the day, and on steamy evenings you could see the night shows they put on there, always ending with a gigantic fireworks display. There were plenty of ballfields and picnic grounds, rowboats on the lake, and roller and ice skating in the cavernous old New York City Building.

One summer they closed down my "backyard." A big fence was erected around the site and a Pinkerton guard told me the swimming pool was closed. So were the skating rinks. And the ballfields. They had taken all of this away so they could have a World's Fair in my backyard.

My parents and my teachers said it would be wonderful, but I wasn't convinced. On an August afternoon in 1962 I snuck through a portion of a gate to see for myself what they were doing to my park. It did look interesting, all of those strange shapes growing up around the old familiar streets. A severe cloudburst interrupted my exploration right in the middle of the construction site, and a Pinkerton "paddy wagon" picked me up. The guard gave me a good scare and threatened to have me arrested if he ever caught me in there again. "This time I'll let you go," he said as he dropped me off, soaked with mud, by the Fair's offices. Just then another Pinkerton guard called from the doorway—"Hey kid, over here!" As I thought about making a quick getaway, he

---

This essay is taken from a feature article that appeared in the *Flushing Tribune*, August 6–12, 1981.

moved toward me. "I was just leaving, really," I pleaded. But he took me by the arm into the building, into a large office that certainly looked important—and foreboding.

An elderly man (I figured he was the guards' boss) said he had seen me from his window, and that I looked wet: "What were you doing here?" he wanted to know. I said I lived in the projects and that they closed down my park and I wanted to see for myself what was going on. He smiled warmly, put me at ease, and told his secretary to get me a hot chocolate. He asked me to sit down, and he asked me about the Bland projects, about my school. He told me that the park would be given back after the Fair was over, and that it would be even bigger and better than before. And he said he hoped I would really like the Fair.

He had his secretary give me some pictures of what the Fair would look like "so that you won't come back until it's open—you really could get hurt out there." He shook my hand and told his secretary to take my address. Shortly after that I received an invitation to a ground-breaking ceremony. I got permission to take off from school and nervously went back to the Fair office building. There, to my astonishment, the old man was walking with John F. Kennedy, the President of the United States. In my backyard.

After he had shown a model of the Fair to the President, the old man came up to me and said, "Here's my friend from the neighborhood." We remained friends, until, at the age of 92, Robert Moses died.

The Valley of Ashes

In 1932, down in the Valley of Ashes, Robert Moses surveyed the bleak terrain of forty years' accumulation of dirt and offscourings, piled high over the swampy meadow. To most men the vast dismal mosquito-ridden swamp was a hopeless, arid, hellish place that would forever be the dumping ground of the metropolis. With the exception of a local band of shanty dwellers who made their living by trapping and selling the many fur-bearing animals that haunted the meadow, most people avoided the area like the plague. But not Robert Moses.

The Valley of Ashes had inspired the poetic imagination of author F. Scott Fitzgerald a decade before, when, in his novel *The Great Gatsby,* he described the Corona Dumps:

> About half way between West Egg and New York the motor road hastily joins the railroad and runs beside it for a quarter of a mile, so as to shrink away from a certain desolate area of land. This is a valley of ashes. . . .

Later the dumps inspired the creative imagination of Robert Moses who trudged through them and witnessed not an expanse of gray ashes, but acres of green fields. Where workmen were unloading trainloads of junk and debris he saw ballfields and picnic grounds. Making his way around the great mountain of ashes he came upon the foul, muddy waterway and saw in its place a lake with boaters and fishermen along banks of fresh, clear water. As Moses pored over maps of the area he saw the site was twice the size of Central Park and, more important, it was located in almost the exact geographic center of New York City, in an area where the population center of the city was steadily shifting.

But Moses' vision did not end at Flushing Meadow. Above the meadow, to the north along the path of the great glacier was a terminal moraine, which if preserved and set aside could become a continuous chain of parks, in the English "greensward" tradition. The links could connect Flushing Meadows at one end with another tidal basin, Alley Pond, at the other. Between the two would be the Kissena Corridor, Kissena Park, Cunningham Park, and the old Vanderbilt Motor Parkway. This chain would make New York's largest expanse of greenery, six miles long from Meadow to Meadow, extending to the city border. This vision had fascinated Moses for a number of years, but the obstacles to the reclamation of the Meadow were overwhelming, physically and financially. The acquisition and landscaping of the Corona dump remained but a dream.

By 1933 Moses had just completed the building of the great new Triborough Bridge, and was looking for a connection between the bridge and the parkway system of Eastern Long Island. The route led inevitably along Flushing Bay, through the Meadow and the middle of the dump. The meadow had been bisected by a few ill-constructed causeways. At least two plank bridges had collapsed on the main causeway as traffic increased. In order to meet mounting local opposition and to raise property values in anticipation of possible condemnation, "Fishhooks" McCarthy, the owner of the Brooklyn Ash Removal Company, established a dubious golf course in one corner of the dump, which according to Moses, had "all the pathetic beauty and frailty of a single rose in a dung heap."

Meanwhile, the state prepared to build the proposed parkway and the city to acquire the land. It was found that the city already owned patches of the meadow where water supply wells had been sunk and sealed for future use. Negotiations had been started to buy out the Brooklyn Ash Disposal Company and end the dumping. It became necessary to conclude complicated negotiations to buy the dump, pay for disposal plants which the company had built for the city, and to settle for equipment. However, the state would only work within an ordinary parkway right of way. The artery would be driven, therefore, through the desolation in the form of a chute, with the great mountains of ash and refuse on either side. Moses did not like the idea of landscaping these monsters, and felt that the only answer would be to acquire the entire meadow, clean up the Bay, and establish a great park on the site. Depite Moses' impressive arguments for this, it remained only a dream; there was no sign of money in the offing, and many more pressing projects were making demands in those hard times.

It took a Belgian engineer, Joseph Shagden, and his daughter, both from Kew Gardens, Queens, to make the dream possible. Shagden proposed the idea of a New York World's Fair and Moses leaped at it—provided the Fair rose on one site only, the 1,216 acres along Flushing Bay. Moses sold the idea to Mayor Fiorello LaGuardia and began the monumental building task.

By the fall of 1936 the ash-gray men with leaden spades were nowhere to be seen among the acres of Flushing Meadows. In their place had come men with slide rules and blueprints and visions of a Meadow reclaimed. By night and day the massive construction crew carried out the work of transforming a municipal eyesore into a meeting place of nations.

The first step was to level the dump by spreading it over a large part of the meadow, digging out much of it for two lakes of 146 acres and processing this muck to make topsoil to spread over the ashes and refuse. It became necessary to prepare an entirely new drainage plan for the area surrounding the Flushing Meadow. With the construction of two lakes and a great tide dam across the River, all such drainage into the lake area had to stop. Storm water had to be run directly into the Bay. All of the old plans for city drainage had to be discarded and new ones adopted. A new drain was created, as large as a tube of the Holland Tunnel. The city's sewer plans for the area which were progressing slowly were speeded up and a huge plan started at Tallman's Island on the East River.

Within a short period of time, the decomposition of sludge on the bay bottom had ended, the generation of gas stopped and the atmosphere was cleared of hydrogen sulphide. Along the Bay a great sea wall was built and a boat basin created. The dumping was stopped at Rikers Island. The fires were put out and the great mountains of refuse were removed. A temporary IND subway spur was built running from the south end of the Meadow, along the Lake into the heart of the fairgrounds. A new IRT and Long Island Railroad station was created with a pedestrian overpass leading directly into the grounds. The rapid transit lines and public streets and arteries leading into the Meadow were improved and expanded. Great under- and over passes were constructed to carry the main arteries across the Fair, to separate through traffic from local, and to make the Meadow safe for pedestrians. The Grand Central Parkway was constructed through the Meadow, and a great Cloverleaf of the Future connected it with the new World's Fair Boulevard (today known as Horace Harding Expressway). As a part of the Fair improvement, Moses coordinated his two agencies, the city Parks Department and the Triborough Bridge & Tunnel Authority, in a program of basic improvements in the area. One of these was construction of a new bridge over the East River connecting the Bronx and Queens. The Whitestone Bridge was completed and opened on April 29, 1939, the day before the opening of the Fair.

Because the creation of the World's Fair site had the ultimate goal of bringing forth a great new city park, the Fair plans called for a bold wedding of architecture with horticulture. The task of filling and grading involved moving 50,000,000 cubic yards of ash fill. Within 190 working days the large force of men and machinery were able to establish a new, porous subsoil. This was brought about while workers fought violent upheavals in the meadow mat, called "mud waves. Finally, when the topsoil was ready, acres of lawns were created throughout the site and 10,000 mature tress planted on the grounds. These, though imported from around the world, soon set themselves into an environment which was, to a large extent, synthetic. Tens of thousands of flowers of all varieties were planted. What had been, but a short time before, a dismal, melancholy, tidal marsh, had now been transformed into a panorama of boulevards integrated and ornamented by lawns, shade trees, shrub masses, bright flower patterns and shimmering lagoons. Even to those who lived along the rim of the vast meadow and had been privileged to see the transformation with their own eyes, it was nonetheless a Miracle.

After the Fair

The 1939 World's Fair was a popular and aristic success, but World War II interrupted Moses' plans for a great recreational-cultural complex at Flushing Meadows. After the war it was Moses who was instrumental in bringing the United Nations to New York City. While he engineered the construction of its permanent headquarters on the East River in Manhattan, he set up a temporary meeting place in the New York City Building at Flushing Meadows, left from the 1939 World's Fair. There the UN remained from 1946–1950.

Despite budgetary restrictions, Moses never abandoned his initial vision of a great park system extending from Flushing Meadows to Alley Pond at the city border. But monumental projects awaited him, not only in other parts of the city but in other parts of the state as well. It was 1964, twenty-five years since New York held its last World's Fair, before Moses saw an opportunity to complete his dream of a great park at Flushing Meadows. And that is what brought him to my backyard.

On June 3, 1967 Moses' thirty-year dream had come true as he handed a restored and completed Flushing Meadows-Corona Park back to the city's Parks Department following its use as the site of the second New York World's Fair. But Moses sensed that his days of power were drawing to a close and he suspected that the Lindsay administration would ignore this great new resource in favor of chic "happenings" in Manhattan parks. Over the next twelve years, after Governor Rockefeller reorganized the Triborough Bridge and Tunnel Authority into the super-agency MTA, Moses appeared to be in retirement, but his energies and talents were busy behind the scenes.

I would meet him periodically over these years and we would discuss current city projects and personalities; he would always ask me how Flushing Meadows Park was doing. You sensed it was one of his proudest achievements, and how saddened he was at the inept maintenance and disregard which the city had for this park. He encouraged me to form a citizens watchdog group to monitor the city's handling of the park. Working with local community planning boards, this group eventually fought the city to obtain such facilities as the Queens Museum and Theater in the Park.

The Last Route

Robert Moses' funeral at St. Peters-by-the-Sea was attended by over 1,000 including Mayor Edward Koch, Governor Hugh Carey, and former Mayor Robert Wagner. But many there remembered a different Moses from the Master Builder of the political scene. Like myself, they remembered an extraordinary visionary and friend. The service was simple, with a brief eulogy in which Moses was quoted as having recently told an old friend, "Never give up the vision. Get on with it." Afterward, the hearse carrying the casket left the scene alone, without police escort, flower cars, or limousines with mourners, not even family members. It drove alone, along the Robert Moses Causeway, west across the Southern State Parkway, onto the Cross Island Parkway and onto the Throgs Neck Bridge—traveling the last route across his creations to a final rest at Woodlawn Cemetery in the Bronx.

Along that route the hearse passed the flags that had been lowered to half staff in Moses' honor by the Mayor. As I drove back from the funeral I noticed two flags at full staff, flying high over Flushing Meadow Park from the two thirty-story flagpoles left from the World's Fair. The flagpole cords had broken a while back so that the flags could not be lowered. Never one for gestures anyway, Moses would have preferred it that way—flags at full staff as a group of kids below played soccer in the grass, and a couple picnicked not far away in this, their backyard. "Don't give up the Vision. Get on with it."

PHOTOGRAPHIC ESSAY

One way of describing the genius of Robert Moses is by pointing to the vision that informed so much of his planning: the vision of open spaces converted to public use. The following pages are offered as evidence, though only partial, of this vision.

J. P. K.

Open Spaces... Public Places...

Heckscher State Park, one of the first Long Island State Parks. Formerly a private estate, it is now a recreation site for millions.

Courtesy of the Long Island State Parks Commission

Open Spaces . . . Public Places . . .

Jones Beach State Park, Long Island's South Shore, probably the fullest achievement of Moses' vision of a vast public-use area.

Courtesy of the Long Island State Parks Commission

Open Spaces . . . Public Places . . .

A view north of Robert Moses State Park and Robert Moses Causeway, Long Island. Another State Park in Massena bears the same name, tributes, all, to the "Master Builder."

Courtesy of the Long Island State Parks Commission

Open Spaces . . . Public Places . . .

Golf course at Bethpage State Park, Long Island. Considered one of the finest in the nation, the course welcomes players at any level of proficiency.

Courtesy of the Long Island State Parks Commission

Open Spaces... Public Places...

The Club House at Bethpage State Park, Long Island, as it appeared in 1936. Designs in autos have changed, but the Club House retains much of its original charm.

Courtesy of the Long Island State Parks Commission

Open Spaces . . . Public Places . . .

Headquarters of the Long Island State Park Commission, Belmont Lake State Park. The administration of public land imposes its own spatial demands, for which the former estate of August Belmont amply provides. The Headquarters was a Moses addition.

Courtesy of the Long Island State Parks Commission

Open Spaces . . . Public Places . . .

A hiking path at Wildwood State Park, Wading River, Long Island.

Courtesy of Nassau County Museum Reference Library

Valley Stream State Park is still an oasis, though no longer so idyllic, amid the heavily populated suburbs.

Courtesy of Nassau County Museum Reference Library

Open Spaces... Public Places...

Part of the original signage at Jones Beach State Park (with an original lamppost in the background); this could almost be the emblem of another Moses' creation, the Long Island Expressway—a public place too often "over populated" with cars.

Courtesy of Nassau County Museum Reference Library

Open Spaces . . . Public Places . . .

Captree Bridge, later renamed for Robert Moses. One of many built by him to connect portions of Long Island's barrier beaches for greater access.

Courtesy of Nassau County Museum Reference Library

Hither Hills State Park, Montauk. Another of the early park sites on Long Island, it now offers camping facilities for owners of recreational vehicles.

Courtesy of Nassau County Museum Reference Library

Needed for access to these public places are roadways—"parkways" Moses called them.

A portion of the Southern State Parkway.

Courtesy of the Long Island State Parks Commission

and bridges—

View from the Brooklyn tower of the Verrazano Narrows Bridge.

Copyright, Jim Cummins, New York Newsday, 1985

leading to places of recreation—

Sailboats at rest. Part of the Heckscher State Park fleet available for public use.

Courtesy of the Long Island State Park Commission

places of recreation—

Shea Stadium, Flushing. The Stadium enfolds two American passions, automobiles and baseball, in one large embrace.

Courtesy of Queens Public Library

of exploration—

1939 World's Fair, Flushing Meadows, where the future took shape before wondering eyes.

Courtesy of Queens Public Library

1964 World's Fair, on the same site, was Robert Moses' "last hurrah."

Courtesy of Queens Public Library

—*and of inspiration.*

Montauk Point State Park.

Courtesy of the Long Island State Parks Commission

"The wild unrest, the snowy, curling caps . . .
Seeking the shores forever."
    Walt Whitman, "From Montauk Point."

NASSAU AND SUFFOLK COUNTIES

Courtesy of Nassau County Museum Reference Library

Jones Beach Theatre with parking lots and water tower in distance.

The Building of Jones Beach*
Robert Moses

Jones Beach began in 1924 with a remote little ol' makeshift state park of two hundred acres on Fire Island required to house passengers suspected of having cholera on board a stranded ship off shore. There were five commissioners, who each had a $1,500 a year deputy. What the commissioners and the deputies did, I don't know. The Federal government owned all the accreted land on Fire Island, west of the lighthouse, and four townships, two in Nassau and two in Suffolk, were the owners of Jones Beach.

Let us have no illusions about Jones Beach as we found it. It was an isolated, swampy sand bar accessible only by small boats and infrequent ferries, inhabited by fishermen and loners, surf casters and assorted oddballs, and beach combers trying to get away from it all. Encompassing meadows were traditionally used for cutting salt hay for cattle. The tales told of a lovely, primitive, paradised wilderness with indestructible dunes were fiction. Our concept of matchless shore front public recreation park open to everyone was still generally regarded by the natives with suspicion and dislike.

We opened the park in 1929 in a sand storm, after I borrowed money from my mother to pay busted contractors. The dedication took place before we finished Beach West. The sand storm knocked out carburetors in thousands of cars whose passengers said the whole thing was a fiasco and nobody would ever come there again. Jones Beach was, in fact, a mosquito-infested tidal swamp full of stagnant pools flanked by shifting dunes. We filled and planted on it every shrub that would grow in sandy soil. The barrier beach was developed in the face of bitter, unreasoning,

---

*This is a transcript of a tape recorded talk given by Robert Moses on February 26, 1974 at a meeting of the Freeport Historical Society. The tape is part of the collections of the Nassau County Museum Reference Library located in the Long Island Studies Institute, Axinn Library, at Hofstra University.

vindictive, personal opposition and classic removal from office. We fought the equinoctial storms, the local Ku Klux Klan, baymen, cottagers who loved their isolation, and rumrunners who had no use for authorities. We did, however, establish rapport with the bootleggers who had twenty mile an hour skiffs powered by airplane engines, and in our regular poker games with the lighthouse keepers we could order anything up to and including champagne. For two years on the Babylon commuter trains nobody spoke to me; the porter was horrified when I strayed into the Islip club car, and ordered me out.

Ellison's Hotel, a combination of bath, bar, and cat-house, stood stubbornly in our way and the Town of Hempstead. Ellison attempted to stop the entire Jones Beach program. He held up our engineers and contractors before we had clear title from the township. We beat him, and forced him to take his shacks elsewhere. He moved to the Meadowlands, which we took later on when we built the loop from Jones Beach to Long Beach, and that was the end of Ellison.

The Selah Strong case, to decide whether there was still private ownership of part of the Oyster Bay Beach, went all the way to the United States Supreme Court.[1] A Guggenheim game refuge blocked our way.[2] These so-called sportsmen paid the Town of Oyster Bay an annual tender of $500 an acre for fifty acres on a procure fifteen-year lease. Babylon's claim to ownership of the entire land under water was brought to a finish, and it was town beach land for a state park and a right of way for our Ocean Parkway.[3] Judge Cooper, a bitter opponent who owned the influential Babylon *Leader*, was a member of the town board and himself a proclaimer to beach land.[4]

Close friendly relations with Wilbur Doughty, the Republican boss of Nassau, and his top political deputies, including Russel Sprague, was a tremendous asset. Our greatest friend was Douglas Smith who had known Wilbur at the Fulton Fishmarket and as an Assemblyman in Albany.

In those troublesome days the regional plan of New York vigorously opposed our program, and even advocated splitting up Jones Beach into minute subdivisions and selling them to cottagers. They brought into the picture, from abroad, Thomas Adams, a distinguished British planner, Chief Advisor to the London County Council; and years later Mr. Adams, a Scot with a conscience, admitted his mistake and congratulated me on the success of our program. This is verbatim what he said:

> Fifteen years ago you and I walked up Fourth Ave. and you told me that you had little patience with plans that did not lead to action. Since then you have been responsible for remarkable work in New York, and by this time must have become rather blase toward appreciating words. Perhaps, however, an expression of the congratulations and admiration from one who had differences of view may startle you into feeling that it is based on real sincerity. No doubt I was too strong willed in holding my views, and perhaps you were somewhat over intolerant of my ideas that failed to register into immediate action. My comparatively small efforts ended when yours began, for the record of your achievement has made you widely and deservedly know. I wish it were in the realm of possibility that you could come to London and, by a mere recital of what you have done in New York, inspire the city fathers into doing something, let me emulate your work. As my connection with New York has long ceased, I have no object in writing to you except to offer these congratulations, and to express the hope that there are no remnants of bitterness between us regarding past differences. I hope to inspect some of your work when I next visit New York.[5]

In a *Newsday* column of May 21, 1966, entitled "Jones Beach After Forty Years," I said, in substance, "Back in 1925, Sid Shapiro, then a chief engineer, was running a little survey party from a shack upon a high hill on Jones Beach. The Coast Guard crew and our adopted hermit, Will Cuppy, were our neighbors; so were abandoned, vicious wild cats and dogs, scores of rabbits, and one family of red foxes. Not to speak of clamdiggers, most of whom had not seen New York in twenty years and had no idea of ever returning. At one stage of the game, the Albany auditor called off Sid's funds because he was surveying beyond the tidal line mentioned in the appropriation bill. Sid's engineers were starving, and some of us personally brought food to keep them alive. Almost nobody in those days believed in Jones Beach.

Here are two editorials, years apart, from the *New York Herald Tribune*. There was never a decent apology for the first, nor an explanation of what caused this change of heart. The *Herald Tribune* on Saturday, November 14, 1925: "In overwhelmingly rejecting the program to turn over Jones Beach to the Long Island

State Park Commissioner, the voters of the Town of Hempstead delivered a deserved rebuke to that blundering body. Now come the proposals for the Nassau and Suffolk Park Commissions to handle the development of beaches and other playgrounds, and there is an excellent prospect that Long Island is on the way to escaping from the clutches of a Moses Commission, and will before long begin the sound park development that is so greatly needed."

In the same paper, on Monday, August 21, 1933, came an editorial entitled "Four Years of Jones Beach:" "A few days late, perhaps (but the anniversaries of bathing beaches are seldom announced with cake and candle), we congratulate Jones Beach and the people of the State of New York upon its fourth birthday. There is, to our knowledge, nothing of its kind as fine as Jones Beach anywhere in the world. Millions of New Yorkers who have derived health and pleasure from its facilities, both natural and artificial, will probably agree with us, no matter how few the order of lesser world's public beaches they may have seen." It is quite a change.

Our difficulties at Fire Island were similar to those of Jones Beach. Harold Phelps Stokes, a Yale classmate of mine, persuaded Herbert Hoover, then Secretary of Commerce, to give us Fire Island west of the lighthouse. Personal friendship, not super duper planning did this. Our original plans for the reclamation and elevation of the Jones Beach and Fire Island barriers on the Ocean Parkway were ridiculed until they began to attract visitors in 1929. The planting of trees, shrubs, and grass that would grow in sandy soil was called absurd, but most of it endured.

We owed much of our accomplishments to a succession of devoted, dedicated, unpaid commissioners, headed today by Holly Patterson, who has been around almost as long as I have, engineers such as Arthur Howland, Earl Andrews, Ken Morton, Stanley Pollack, and Sid Shapiro. For our Council, Ray McNulty and Frank Doherty, my secretary, Hazel Tappen. And now we have Hawthorn Bill as chief of staff, a worthy successor to the early executives. The future of Jones Beach and Fire Island are sure.

Protective works to prevent beach erosion are still and always will be necessary. There is room for more bath houses and parking on state and federal land. The road east of Fire Island from the lighthouse to the natural seashore must be built because without it only 20% of those demanding recreation can be accommodated. We have established high standards of upkeep and they have been maintained to this day. We have demonstrated that the public beach could be run for the benefit of 95% of good people and not surrender to 3 or 4% of bums. And of course the demands of the future will dictate changes. One who has at the same time operated city, suburban, and exurban parks, can testify to the differences and objectives of visitors. There are policemen and firemen who want to get out of town for a day of fishing in the open boats off Captree to preserve their sanity. There are gregarious, compacted Bronx families, loaded down with incredible paraphernalia, who can't bear to be far apart from, while outdoors, what they have indoors at home. There will be much more year-round usage as we magnify the sun's rays and phase out the wind. I remember when bathers had to wear tops to escape arrest; today the only punishable offense is stark nudity.

You see, the destructionists did us a great favor because they unwittingly made us more stubborn, hidebound, and bullet proof. Vision, persistence, and luck saved us at least as much as nobility of purpose. Last Sunday the Players Club in New York put on a festival, or a revival, as a matter of fact, of *South Pacific*, which brought back memories of the many splendid outdoor shows thousands have enjoyed at Jones Beach under the constellations and overlooking the Atlantic. For more than forty years *afficionados* of all ages have marked time to the music, sung the words to Rodgers and Hammerstein's unforgettable melodies, and have thanked Guy Lombardo, Mike Todd, and other beach impressarios, and celebrated the architecture of Aymar Embury and Gilmore Clark.

Here it is in a nutshell. An example of planned, imaginative, persistent, nonpolitical public enterprise. This is conservation in a broader sense, before the three "E's" of ecology, environmentalism, ecesitics, became slogans of extremists and crusaders. When the critics tell you that there has been nothing but neglect of the great outdoors, take them to Jones Beach and Fire Island and tell them to look around about them.

EDITOR'S NOTES

1. On the Oyster Bay lawsuits, see Chester R. Blakelock, "History of Long Island State Parks," in *Long Island: A History of Two Great Counties, Nassau and Suffolk,* edited by Paul Bailey (New York: Lewis Historical Publishing Co., 1949), II: 282–283.

2. The reference is to a group of wealthy sportsmen headed by Solomon Guggenheim who had a duck-hunting preserve on 500 acres of meadowland owned by the Town of Oyster Bay. See Caro, p. 233.

3. For the story of the Babylon Township claim, see Caro, pp. 237–38.

4. Judge James B. Cooper. See Caro, pp. 236–37.

5. Moses appears to be reading from a letter here, the whereabouts of which the editor has not established.

Robert Moses: Long Island's First Environmentalist

John A. Black

Virtually every environmental problem presently plaguing Long Island, and indeed, all urban and suburban areas, was recognized long ago by Robert Moses. His biographer, Robert Caro, accurately recounts Moses' vision in planning and developing the Long Island park and parkway system and notes that Moses believed Long Island would remain a recreational area for New York City's masses. Then, however, he discounts Moses' accomplishments and blames him for Long Island's suburbanization and all of its subsequent environmental ills. In reality, had Moses' concepts and recommendations been fully heeded and implemented, many of these problems would not have occurred. In order to evaluate Moses fairly it is necessary to fully examine his activities, plans, and recommendations.

Undoubtedly Moses' major accomplishment was the development of the state's parks and parkway system. His parkways, however, did much more than carry recreation seekers to and from parks. Rather, Moses insisted on a right-of-way of unprecedented width.[1] The right-of-way was well landscaped, making each parkway itself a ribbon park, so that even as people were driving to parks, they were driving through parks.[2] Moreover, Moses planned the parkways for limited access to prevent the random development so commonly found along roadways with unlimited curb cuts. Moses, "instead of building an ordinary road . . . lined with all kinds of objectionable shacks and signs . . . planned to build a parkway with very infrequent access."[3] Limited access proved to be the major reason that the dunes and bay-side salt marshes along Jones Beach have been preserved and that random development has not occurred. One need only compare the aesthetic drive along this barrier beach to the one along Rockaway, Long Beach or Westhampton Beach to see the protection afforded by a limited access parkway. Even along roadless Fire Island the unrestricted use of off-the-road vehicles has wrought greater havoc to the dunes and beach, and has opened this island to more random development than the millions of autos that traverse the Ocean Parkway on Jones Beach.[4] Thus, very early in his career, Moses had learned the secret of providing access while simultaneously preserving large sections of a fragile barrier beach.

Moses also knew the crucial difference between refuges and recreational areas and realized that it was unrealistic, if not impossible, to expect to limit access to all of the state's natural areas with a huge city on its doorstep. Rather, as President of the Long Island Park Commission, he opted for a balance between recreation and open space. As a result, Valley Stream, Hempstead Lake, Belmont, Heckscher and Montauk State Parks provide open space and active recreation as does Jones Beach and Sunken Meadow. Connetquot and Nissequogue River State Parks, on the other hand, were acquired by Moses to serve as limited access preserves.[5]

Moses also attempted to acquire virtually the entire Montauk "peninsula" from Napeague Harbor eastward to Montauk Point and intended that Gardiners Island be acquired as well. He anticipated for these a balanced mix of land use: the mainland portions would be used for active recreation such as swimming, hiking, camping, etc.; Gardiners Island was to be a limited access preserve. He also intended to acquire a large portion of the Orient "peninsula." Thus, Moses planned that vast areas on the tips of both of Paumanok's flukes would be in public ownership.[6]

Unfortunately, he encountered both indifference and strong opposition. Much of the property he wished to acquire belonged to a private developer and a holding company consisting of the Long Island Rail Road and

> . . . the Standard Oil Pratts. The ambitious beleagured, despised Long Island State Park Commission set out to make 8,000 acres of Montauk a public reservation, protected against encroachment and subdivisions, eventually to include all of Gardiners Island's 3,000 acres and, considerable portion of Orient Point. It was a noble dream.[7]

Some 50 years ago, there was virtually no public support for these acquisitions. Moses, however, persisted and the "land battle finally ended with a state park of 1,800 acres at Hither Hills and 700 at the Point, not bad considering our poverty and the opposition. . . ."[8] The Hither Hills acquisition included the ecologically unique Moving Dune area, and "the Point," to which Moses refers, included the sand spit at Orient Point which had been acquired in 1929 and became Orient Point State Park.

To provide access to the Montauk properties Moses planned to span Fire Island Inlet and to continue the Jones Beach Ocean Parkway along Fire Island and Westhampton Beach. The parkway would then cross Shinnecock Bay at Hampton Bays and continue along the shore to Montauk Point. State parks were to be developed to the east of Point O'Woods, Smith Point and Quogue.[9] The extension of the Ocean Parkway was opposed, initially in the 1930s on economic grounds and then, in the 1960s, by the environmental movement.[10] Had Moses been successful, a limited access parkway would have prevented the over-development, mismanagement, and virtual destruction of Westhampton Beach. It would also have prevented the random development on all of Fire Island and the destruction of the dunes on the eastern portion of that island due to the unregulated use of off-the-road vehicles in the Smith Point County Park.

Moses was also solely responsible for the preservation of Jamaica Bay and the establishment of the Jamaica Bay Wildlife Refuge. In the early 1900s, New York City, under the aegis of the Jamaica Bay Improvement Commission, planned to develop this area into an industrial port and ship terminal. By 1922 the city had adopted plans

> . . . under which the water and the marshlands . . . were to be blotted out by two islands . . . a system of navigation channels, boarded by mile after mile of industrial piers and warves. A quarter of a billion cubic yards of fill was to be dredged to make the islands . . . the completed Jamaica Bay port would be greater than the combined ports of Liverpool, Rotterdam and Hamburg.[11]

Moses was opposed to the entire plan and particularly objected to the proposal to use a portion of the area for the disposal of municipal solid waste. He asked Mayor Fiorello LaGuardia: "Having spent millions to remove two great dumps at Flushing Bay . . . are we so stupid as to fill up the middle of Jamaica

Bay with garbage, rubbish and ashes?"[12] Ultimately, Moses was successful in blocking this billion dollar project and "rescued the bay with all its meadowlands and islands and made it into the largest bird refuge in any city in the world—10,000 acres."[13]

Moses had little faith in "creative" methods of land acquisition such as today's transfer of development rights, farmland preservation strategies, etc. He believed that if land was to be acquired it should be either donated outright or purchased at a fair market price.

> If the state, county and town people really want them, take them. They won't get them by trick zoning and tax gimmicks. If permanent parks are the objective, buy or condemn open woodland and shore and then let the realtor and farmer compete for the rest.[14]

When one considers the scale of the Long Island State Park Commission's acquisitions, it is obvious that Moses' methods were effective. Between 1924 when he was appointed the first president of the Commission and the mid-1930s, the property for Valley Stream, Hempstead Lake, Heckscher, Hither Hills, Montauk, Sunken Meadow, Orient Point, Jones Beach and Fire Island State Parks was acquired, as well as the right-of-way for much of Wantagh, Southern, and Northern State Parkways. Later the Connetquot and Nissequogue River Preserves, Bayard Cutting Arboretum, Caumsett State Park, etc., were added to the park system. This was a truly remarkable accomplishment when compared to the snail's pace of public acquisition since then.

In addition to the acquisition of land and the development of the State's park and parkway system, Moses was also concerned with a variety of environmental problems. It is important to note that Moses foresaw these problems on the horizon long before they were recognized as environmental problems. On August 18, 1931 Moses addressed the National Shellfish Association and noted that the major problems confronting baymen were ineffective planning, poor zoning and building practices, the population increase along the shoreline, and liquid and solid waste.[15]

In the course of this address Moses noted that the Long Island State Park Commission was committed to the preservation of the wetlands under their jurisdiction and also to the protection of the coastal waters "for recreation . . . and for your shellfish and fishing generally . . . ."[16]

Moses was also an active opponent of sand and gravel operations and uncontrolled dredging projects. These operations were common shorefront activities from Port Washington to Port Jefferson in the early 1900s. Moses believed that these activities provided only a very transitory benefit to the community in terms of employment. After the woodlands had been destroyed and the hills leveled the operation would move elsewhere, leaving a plundered landscape and depressed property values. Hydraulic dredging of the north shore harbors was equally harmful and destroyed harbor bottom, wetlands, and fin and shellfish. Since these operations generated large profits, Moses recognized the futility of relying on local zoning and other laws to regulate these activities.[17]

The battle to regulate these operations was led by J. C. Byars, the editor of *The County Review*, which was published in Riverhead. Moses "added his voice and the influence of his commission . . ." in the autumn of 1930.[18] Known as the best bill drafter in Albany, Moses put his talents to use by drafting legislation to regulate the mining operations.[19] It was Moses' contention that it was "essential to control these operations . . . under authorization of a special act of the legislature. . . ."[20] These operations were eventually controlled decades later, but only after large areas of Long Island had been carted away by the sand and gravel companies.

Although Moses originally believed that Long Island would remain a rural area and intended that it would provide open space and recreational opportunities for city dwellers, by the mid-1930s he did foresee its eventual population growth and suburbanization and urged that this be recognized and planned for.[21] His recommendations were, however, for the most part, unheeded; "we were distant, muffled voices crying in the wilderness and little regarded at the time."[22]

Moses was a strong proponent of zoning as a means of assuring the orderly growth of Long Island. In the mid-1930s he was appointed to the Nassau County Charter Commission. The Commission was particularly concerned that a community would use its zoning powers to direct undesirable industry toward its far borders adjacent to a neighboring community. To rectify this potential abuse the Charter Commission required that the rezoning of any land within 300 feet of another community must be reviewed by the Nassau County Planning Commission.[23]

So successful was this provision that Moses used the precedent to require that the Long Island Park Commission review any zoning changes within 500 feet of a state park or parkway. This provision enabled the Long Island State Park Commission to more effectively control development adjacent to the right-of-way of its parkways and to more effectively maintain their characteristics as ribbon parks. Moreover, it discouraged the development of amusement parks, food stands, etc., so often seen outside of the national parks.

Moses also foresaw the consequences of uncontrolled development along Westhampton Beach. In 1938 he warned that the character of the barrier beach would be destroyed by residential and commercial development in the absence of meaningful zoning and building codes.[24] His warnings were completely ignored. Thus, when the memories of the Hurricane of 1938 had faded and the wartime building moratorium was lifted, Dune Road, with its unlimited access did spur uncontrolled development which has fostered all of today's problems on that barrier island.[25]

As Long Island continued to develop in the post-war years Moses was, once again, a voice in the wilderness when he asked for more effective zoning. He noted that the "process of subdivision is often unscrupulous, shocking and larcenous."[26] Moses anticipated the land-use controls recommended by the Long Island Regional Planning Board in 1978, which attempted to prevent the further degradation of groundwater, when he stated that the "answers are bigger residential plots, smaller building coverage. . . ."[27]

In 1970, when opposing the rezoning of large north shore areas, Moses noted that "you can't promote ecology by subdivision . . . the postage stamp subdivisions have their appendages which also show up vacant open space, for example the shopping centers. . . ."[28] For over four decades Moses fought for improved zoning but was largely ignored. Even today while elected officials tout strengthened zoning and grandiose master plans with one hand, they grant variances with the other.

Moses was far ahead of his time when, in 1934, he recognized the inadequacies of the existing wastewater collection systems. It was common practice to collect both sewage and storm water in the same lines. Even during periods of moderate rainfall these systems overloaded the already stressed treatment plants. Moses believed these collection systems were obsolete and felt that they should be eliminated. Moreover, he proposed that plants be expressly constructed to treat storm water.[29] This is remarkable, since the effect of storm water as a major contaminant was not generally recognized until the 1970s, when the Long Island Regional Planning Board undertook the area-wide water management planning study.[30] To date, however, storm water is not treated, nor have combined collection systems been eliminated in many communities.

Although Moses was an early advocate of sewer treatment plants he was a critic of the Southwest Sewer District. He believed that Suffolk County was rushing toward construction with inadequate study and so urged caution. He recommended that an advisory board of recognized experts be appointed to develop a comprehensive plan. More important, he apparently recognized the technical flaws in the Southwest Sewer District long before anyone else. "You cannot take a defective . . . system and extend and piece it out as if you were adding a few miles to an existing road.[31]

The wisdom of Moses' words proved true in 1976 when the Blue Ribbon Committee on Technical Aspects of the Southwest Sewer District found major flaws in the system.[32] By then, however, the County was committed to the construction of a billion-dollar plant that would deplete the aquifer and adversely affect the lakes, streams, ponds and rivers from Amityville to Great River.[33]

Moses was also concerned with the fragmented approach that both counties were taking toward the management of liquid and solid waste. He recommended that a single agency be established "to avoid haphazard remedies and prevent further . . . pollution."[34] Had he been aware of resource recovery and the codisposal of sludge, it is probable that he would have favored these methods of dealing with municipal solid waste and sludge while generating electricity. Moses did fail to predict the transport of municipal solid waste from Long Island, however. "Recently there has been much bally hoo about shipping garbage at night by rail to outlying areas . . . This is almost too silly for comment."[35] His comments on the garbage barge of the summer of 1987 would be interesting!

As Long Island continued to develop, Moses became increasingly concerned with the lack of county parks for the growing population. Recognizing the fact that privately owned golf courses in New York City had long ago been sold to developers, he feared that those in Nassau County would suffer a similar fate. He was also concerned that the remaining north shore estates would be subdivided. To prevent this he recommended that the 35 private golf courses, totaling 5,000 acres and serving but 10,000 golfers, and 10 to 15 estates be acquired. Since these areas were too small to meet the criteria for state parks, Moses suggested that the County undertake the purchase and that they be used for recreation and conservation.[36] He warned that if the acquisition were not carried out, within 10 years fifty percent of the golf courses and virtually all of the estates of 50 or more acres would be subdivided, further exacerbating the county's population increase.[37]

Moses was particularly concerned over the paucity of publicly owned bay front in western Suffolk County. As a result he urged the acquisition of three large bay front properties in the West Islip area." . . . this is a rare opportunity to make a far-sighted public plan in the sole interest of the township and its present and future population . . . it is emphatically not a subject to be left to the tender mercies of realtors. . . ."[38] Although some of this area has been developed, Suffolk County, the Nature Conservancy, and the state did acquire significant acreage in the area.

Moses never quite gave up the hope that Gardiners Island would be preserved and he continually urged its acquisition. He was also an early advocate for the acquisition of Robins Island in Peconic Bay.[39] Presently, both of these properties remain in private ownership with Robins Island in particular jeopardy, since it is in the hands of speculators.

Shortly before his death on July 29, 1981 Robert Moses noted that people "must judge the merits of a project on whether it's done more good than harm."[40] In retrospect, Moses' long record of open space preservation, as a proponent of land-use controls, as an early spokesman for intelligent waste management practices, and as an opponent of subdivision, speaks for itself.

Robert Moses was, undoubtedly, Long Island's first environmentalist.

NOTES

1. Robert Moses, *Public Works: A Dangerous Trade* (N.Y.: McGraw Hill, 1970), p. 113.
2. Robert A. Caro, *The Power Broker: Robert Moses and the Fall of New York* (N.Y.: Alfred A. Knopt, 1974), p. 162.
3. Robert Moses, *Proceedings of the National Shellfish Association*, Chesapeake Biological Laboratory, MD, 1931.
4. John A. Black, "From Fort Tilden to Shinnecock Inlet: The Consequences of Roads and Parkways," *Long Island Forum*, March 1987.
5. Moses, *Public Works*, p. 116.
6. R. Moses, "Montauk Revisited," in From the Bridge, *Newsday*, February 25, 1967.
7. Ibid.
8. Ibid.
9. Moses, *Restoration and Protection of Fire Island*, New York, 1938.
10. Black, "Robert Moses and the Eastern Barrier Beaches," *Long Island Forum*, June 1986.
11. Moses, *The Future of Jamaica Bay*, Department of Parks, City of New York, N.Y. July 18, 1938.
12. Ibid.
13. Moses, "Breezy Point: Fiasco or Treasure" in From the Bridge, *Newsday*, September 17, 1966.
14. Moses, "The Gardiners Bay Preserve," *Newsday*, December 26, 1970.
15. Moses, *Proceedings*, 1931.
16. Ibid.
17. Ibid.
18. Moses, letter to J. C. Byars, Editor, *The County Review*, Riverhead, N.Y., 1930.
19. See "Moses Drafts Law to Curb L. I. Dredges," *County Review*, November 1, 1930.
20. Moses, letter to J. C. Byars.
21. Caro, p. 145.
22. Moses, "Private Golf Courses on Long Island" in From the Bridge, *Newsday*, December 3, 1966.
23. Moses, "Suburban Long Island Zoning" in From the Bridge, *Newsday*, January 7, 1967.
24. Moses, *Restoration and Protection of Fire Island*, New York, 1938.

25. Black, "From Fort Tilden to Shinnecock Inlet: The Consequences of Roads and Parkways," *Long Island Forum,* March 1987.
26. Moses, "Idle Words Won't Beautify Paumanok," *Newsday,* December 13, 1969.
27. Ibid.
28. Moses, "Last Chance for Parks," *Newsday,* July 18, 1970.
29. Moses, *Public Works,* p. 35.
30. Lee E. Koppelman, *The Long Island Comprehensive Waste Treatment Management Plan,* Long Island Regional Planning Board, Hauppauge, N.Y., 1978.
31. Moses, "Suffolk Sanitation: More Study," *Newsday,* October 25, 1969.
32. Black, "Stop the Southwest Sewer District," in Viewpoints, *Newsday,* September 17, 1976.
33. Black, "A Consideration of the Southwest Sewer District," *Implementation of Federal Water Pollution Control Act,* U. S. Government Printing Office, Washington, D.C., 1976.
34. Moses, "Water, Water Everywhere" in From the Bridge, *Newsday,* August 6, 1966.
35. Ibid.
36. Moses, "Private Golf Courses on Long Island."
37. Ibid.
38. Moses, "A Case in Point—The Islip Shorefront," *Newsday,* April 5, 1969.
39. Moses, "The Gardiners Bay Preserve," *Newsday,* December 26, 1970.
40. "Robert Moses Dies at 92, *Newsday,* July 30, 1981.

The Long Island Motor Parkway: Prelude to Robert Moses

Robert Miller

Robert Moses developed a network of roadways which, for better or for worse, dominates the lives of commuters in the metropolitan New York area. Even while suffering in traffic jams on one of these roadways, we have to admire them for the engineering marvels they are and the testimony they offer to Moses' profound faith in the automobile as the key to America's future. But where did Moses get his idea of a parkway, a road designed specifically for the automobile? Was there a precursor to what he devised, and, if so, where?

For the answers to these questions one must turn to the history of a man and an idea, the man, William Kissam Vanderbilt, Jr., and the idea, his conviction—held also by Robert Moses—that America could and should build a better car than any other country in the world.

William K. Vanderbilt was the great grandson of the famous Commodore Cornelius Vanderbilt, consolidator of the upper New York State railway into the New York Central line. Although "Willy K." served his time as president of that railroad, he didn't enjoy it as much as he did racing automobiles. He was a great enthusiast of the "new-fangled" motorcars and loved to race them. He was often troubled, however, by the number of times foreign cars took the trophies in these races. William Vanderbilt believed that America had the materials, manpower, and brains to do a much better job at producing a winning motorcar than it was then doing.

In puzzling over this failure, Vanderbilt remembered his family's credo that competition improved the breed, a belief it had followed in the management of its race horse stables. William decided to sponsor a series of automobile races to further the development of the American automobile through competitive means. In addition to offering several prizes worth a few thousand dollars, he commissioned Louis G. Tiffany to design a large silver trophy, the original model of which is now in the Smithsonian Institution in Washington, D.C.

The races were to be held on Long Island's roads, which, compared with today's, did not offer much. One must remember, however, that the American automobile, in fact, automobiles in general, had only been in existence for about eleven years before the first Vanderbilt race in 1904. Because of natural conditions, Long Island had what the *Automobile Blue Book* called excellent roads, consisting of sand and gravel. The sandy roads might drag at the wheels, but they very seldom allowed the car to sink into muck and mire, and so drivers seldom encountered the huge mud puddles from which cars had to be slowly hauled by a straining team of horses.

Unfortunately for Willy K., the first race was won by a foreign entrant, and the same held true in 1905 and again in 1906. At the 1906 race tragedy struck and one person was killed and four others injured when the crowds refused to stay within barricades erected by the security police. The cars, with their very limited braking ability and extremely hard steering, could not avoid hitting those spectators who broke through onto the roads.

Immediately after the disastrous event Vanderbilt and his associates adjourned to the Garden City Hotel and, a few days later, in downtown Manhattan, formed the Long Island Motor Parkway, Incorporated. Their purpose was to create road use on the Motor Parkway not only for racing but, during the rest of the year, for genuine pleasure driving.

The term "parkway" was already in use, but referred to a tree-lined boulevard or other road leading to a park, such as those designed by Frederick Law Olmsted in the preceding century. The Motor Parkway was to be a different matter; it would connect two distant places with a driveable, hard-surfaced highway absolutely free of grade crossings or interference from anything else, be it trains, horses, or wagons, and it would be completely separate from all local roads. Finally, it was to connect the Queens County line with the Suffolk County seat at Riverhead.

Although pictured in a public relations sketch as a straight line, the Parkway never achieved such perfection. Of course,

Courtesy of Garden City Public Library, Whitten Collection

Westbury Avenue Bridge, 1910

neither did the Long Island Expressway, Northern State Parkway, or any of Robert Moses parkways. Unlike Moses, Vanderbilt could not condemn land for his individual wishes. He had to buy entire farms in many instances, just to get a 100-foot right-of-way. If someone did not agree to sell, Vanderbilt sought someone who would agree; as a result, the road followed what can charitably be called a circuitous route.

By 1908 most of the right-of-way as far as Lake Ronkonkoma had been secured. In the remaining twenty-six miles to Riverhead, trouble arose in the form of farmers who would not sell at what Vanderbilt felt was a reasonable price. Rather than submit to "extortion," he decided to terminate the road at Ronkonkoma.

In the spring of 1908 Vanderbilt was ready to begin construction. On June 6 ceremonies took place just off Jerusalem Avenue in a barren field located in what is now the heart of Levittown. Many speeches were made, chiefly that of Arthur R. Pardington, Vanderbilt's construction vice president recruited from Brooklyn Telephone Company. Vanderbilt was not present, having escaped to his yacht because of troublesome hay fever. Pardington referred to past highways for various kinds of vehicular traffic, canals, railroads, trolleys; now "the day of the automobile has come," he claimed, and a roadway designed just for its use was to be constructed.

Construction was unlike anything we have grown accustomed to in modern road building. No roads existed on which heavy equipment could be moved, nothing large could be dragged along the local roads, no bulldozer was available for removing tree stumps, only horses, men, levers, pulleys, and ropes. When all else failed, the men resorted to blasting powder, a dangerous alternative made even more so by the fact that most of the workers were immigrants who did not understand English.

The road was built with a material brand new to the twentieth century and patented under the name Hassam Paving. It differed from today's concrete in that it was constructed by putting down two layers of heavy crushed stone with reinforcing mesh between the layers. A thin, soupy cement was poured over and between the stones. Once it filled the spaces and a thin layer floated over the top, it was brushed to provide a course, gripping surface. Sand for the cement came initially from Jones Beach, but later Vanderbilt used the bank run sand which comprises most of Long Island's substructure. Limestone for the cement came from the region of the Hudson River Valley.

In order to provide the required amounts of water needed for sanitation and cooking and for cement making, Vanderbilt sank wells, some as deep as 600 feet, all over his property alongside the right-of-way.

Bridge building posed a particular challenge, and there were sixty-five to be erected! Mixing was done on site using stationary boilers and steam-powered mixers. Once forms were erected, concrete was mixed, taken up ramps in wheelbarrows, and poured into the forms. When the forms were removed, the job of installing steelwork began. The bridges were steel I-beams surrounded with concrete and resting on concrete abutments. To get the I-beams in place the men reverted to shipbuilding methods used to step shipmasts in the yard or aboard the vessels. When all beams were positioned molds were built around them and the concrete poured.

The early bridges had only a twenty-three foot span over the roadway, and as time passed and cars were wider, they became traffic hazards. (This was the reason Nassau County removed

Courtesy of Garden City Public Library, Whitten Collection

Construction scars on the Motor Parkway, 1910

them when the Parkway was abandoned.) The sixty-five bridges comprised several different types. The reinforced concrete triple-span overpass at Clinton Road was the largest concrete type. Alley Pond Park in Queens was given a true rarity, a brick-faced reinforced concrete bridge. In Queens, New York City demanded that steel bridges be erected over the main thoroughfares, so Vanderbilt installed what appear to be through, plate-girder bridges, such as those used by railroads, similar to the bridge over the Long Island Rail Road at what is now Bethpage, then called Central Park.

Like Robert Moses, William K. Vanderbilt was concerned for the appearance of the roadway and its surrounding area, and for the provision of those amenities that would make use of his road a true pleasure for motorists. At the time of its construction, and for a while thereafter, the Parkway created quite a scar of fresh earth along its route. This was rectified by landscaping the area, and as the years went by and nature provided help, the Parkway became as one with its surroundings. Vanderbilt was a naturalist and believed in preserving the environment, so that in all senses of the word the Motor Parkway was a very low profile road. One way in which it retained its low profile was the way it hugged the terrain, blending in well with the natural surroundings.

For motorists Vanderbilt provided the Petite Trianon Inn, designed by John Russell Pope, where they could dine in pleasant surroundings on the western shore of Lake Ronkonkoma at the end of their journey. Toll houses, called lodges, were also designed by Pope, who is best known for the Theodore Roosevelt wing of the American Museum of Natural History.

Vanderbilt had hoped the Parkway would pay for itself, through tolls and racing fees as well as usage charges to test automobiles and auto accessories built by the then infant automobile industry which had factories in the East. Unfortunately, the Motor Parkway, which with later additions and improvements reached a final cost of $10 million, never showed a profit. Most American motorists did not have the money to pay the Parkway's tolls, and, following the 1910 race where four people were killed and more than twenty injured, racing car drivers refused to race any longer on a course that took them through crowded public areas. Another blow was dealt when the automobile manufacturers left the East coast for the Great Lakes area to be closer to the source of their steel supply.

As in the case of Moses, Vanderbilt has had his share of critics, some of whom claim he was short-sighted in not having traffic surveys made of the area before building the road to see if it would justify its cost. However, there were only a few thousand cars in the whole country, certainly insufficient numbers to justify paving local streets, much less building long-distance roads. Vanderbilt built the Motor Parkway to propagate the automobile industry and to spur the building and use of automobiles. Considering that it taught the highway industry a great deal about how, as well as how not, to build a modern automobile road, and that it did spur the auto industry to bigger and better things, it was a success.

From 1911, when it was completed, until 1929, with the building of the Moses parkways, Motor Parkway was the only high-speed road to reach the middle of Suffolk County from New York City. After World War I Vanderbilt realized that Americans now had more and better cars, and more money and time to enjoy them. As they used the Parkway in ever greater numbers he attempted to implement a modernization program. He extended

The Long Island Motor Parkway: Prelude to Robert Moses 157

Courtesy of Smithtown Library, Pardington Collection

Meadowbrook Lodge (destroyed c. 1968), 1910

the Parkway westward two and one-half miles to what is now the Long Island Expressway service road and 199th Street in Queens. He also built a feeder road north to Commack in Suffolk County. The Parkway was widened three feet on either side, bringing it from sixteen to twenty-two feet, still too narrow, however, for cars to pass comfortably.

By 1929 Vanderbilt could see the writing on the wall. He went to Robert Moses asking him to buy the Parkway and admitting to Moses his awareness that no one would ride his road for a fee if they could use a public parkway. He pointed out that if Moses bought the road, he could use whatever right-of-way he needed for the new Northern State Parkway and use the rest (old farms and all) for parks, playgrounds, etc. Moses replied that he couldn't use the whole Parkway, just the section between Lakeville Road and New Hyde Park Road. Vanderbilt did not want two disconnected pieces of roadway on his hands and told Moses so. Moses, being Moses, told Vanderbilt to take his offer or he would find the Northern State Parkway paralleling his road entrance for entrance, and that Vanderbilt would end up giving it to Moses and the State for nothing. Vanderbilt left Moses' office and kept the Parkway operating for nine more years, closing it on April 16, 1938. He then deeded the roadway to the counties through which it ran for the $90,000 he owed in back taxes. Moses was correct—they got the Parkway for nothing.

When Queens turned its section of the Motor Parkway into a bicycle and jogging path, Robert Moses was there proudly for the dedication. Nassau County sold most of its portion to the Long Island Lighting Company as power pole rights-of-way. Suffolk County kept thirteen miles of it as a second class road, heavily modernizing it over the years.

There are those who give to the Bronx River Parkway first place among highways designed and built for the automobile, but it was begun three years after the Motor Parkway was completed. The fact that the Bronx River Parkway was a free road as opposed to Vanderbilt's toll road is what clouds the issue, of course, but many of today's inter and intrastate public roads are toll roads, which mitigates the difference considerably. With the exception of the highway divider, cloverleaf and high-speed entrance and exit, everything we have learned about modern superhighway construction has been learned from the Motor Parkway: reinforced concrete pavement, super-elevated curves, limited accessibility, steel reinforced bridges, and elimination of all crossings—all of these came from William K. Vanderbilt's belief, shared later by Robert Moses, in the future of the automobile in America.

In October 1908, the magazine *Automobile* editorialized prophetically, "When its plans are entirely consummated, the Long Island motorway will supply an uninterrupted route across the Island which, owing to its proximity to the metropolis, is destined to be the home of millions with business and social interests in New York City. Someday the state will supply such motorways."

Editors note: the Garden City toll house was moved in March 1989 from its original location on Vanderbilt Court to Seventh Street (east of Franklin Avenue), where it will be headquarters for the Chamber of Commerce and house an exhibit on the Motor Parkway.

Building the Roads to Greatness: Robert Moses and Long Island's State Parkways

J. Lance Mallamo

Recent years have witnessed a tremendous interest in history and historic preservation across the United States. One of the more interesting aspects of this renewed awareness of local and regional heritage has been the identification of sites important to the history and development of recent times, the realization that certain sites, structures and facilities, though built in our own time, have contributed to and changed the course of our destiny far more than anyone would have believed possible at the time they were constructed. Such is the case of Long Island's magnificent State Parkway system, sections of which were determined eligible for the National Register of Historic Places in 1987. This determination officially recognizes the genius of Robert Moses, parkway innovator and acknowledged "Master Builder."

Long Island's parkways originated conceptually as a simple means to move vehicular traffic between the City of New York and the various state parks on Long Island which were under concurrent development by Robert Moses. At the time they were planned and constructed, few would have recognized the implications of such a road system, not only for the face of Long Island, but in the development of specific national policies which resulted in the rise of the American suburb.

The transition of America from a pedestrian to a vehicular society was well underway by the early years of this century. The gracious nineteenth-century avenues, such as New York's "Grand Concourse and Boulevard," located in Bronx County, began to give way to even more ambitious road plans such as the Bronx River Parkway, proposed in 1906, which connected New York City with nearby Westchester County. However, even in the case of the Bronx River, America's first true "park way" designed for automobiles, there was no grand scheme to facilitate traffic patterns. Rather the parkway project was an attempt to gain control of the riverbanks and eradicate pollution sources that had been linked to animal deaths at the Bronx Zoological Park.

By 1909 the concrete paving of Detroit's Woodward Avenue and the start of construction of the Long Island Motor Parkway signaled a change in road building technology that was to revolutionize the manner in which Americans traveled. The Motor Parkway in particular included a number of innovative design features which clearly set it apart from any highway constructed to that time. However, the high toll of the privately owned and operated Motor Parkway precluded most attempts by moderate income automobile owners to traverse the pristine Long Island countryside with ease.

Traditionally, Long Island road corridors had developed over the centuries in a linear fashion, east to west, north to south, often based on ancient Indian trails. Along the three main east-west arteries, North Country, Middle Country, and South Country Roads, various villages had developed, primarily in response to local geographical conditions or perpendicular cross routes. By the 1920s, as automobile production expanded and affordability increased, these major arteries often were clogged with weekend recreational traffic seeking an escape from urban confines. At that time, Long Island's beaches and open spaces were largely closed to non-residents and the local political climate thwarted most attempts to change the status quo.

It was at this time that a peculiar set of opportunities, coupled with the vision and creativity of Robert Moses, led to the creation of a system of State Parks throughout Nassau and Suffolk Counties. Watershed properties in southern Nassau County, acquired years earlier by the then City of Brooklyn, were turned over to the state to form a string of parklands. Moses then turned to the ocean waters at Jones Beach, the rolling fields of Bethpage and the quiet wetlands at Sunken Meadow as sites to develop other major recreational facilities. But the genius of Moses' park plan was not restricted to the park boundaries. To reach these magnificent parks he conceived a comprehensive system of ultra-modern parkways, connecting various parks and recreation areas with the metropolitan New York region. However, these new roadways were to be wider, safer and more beautiful than any road the world had yet seen.

According to Moses' plan the Long Island parkways would not only move traffic, they would provide aesthetic and environmental attributes rarely seen in modern highway construction. While some urged the state to purchase the existing Long Island Motor Parkway, Moses felt that with the cost of acquisition, coupled with the cost of reconstruction to suit contemporary needs, it would be more economical to build new roadways. He correctly foresaw that eventually the Motor Parkway would be turned over to public authorities at no cost in settlement of heavy annual tax payments overdue on the private road.

Perhaps the most significant feature of Moses' Long Island parkway plan was that it was conceived as an integrated system of grade separated roadways traversing Long Island. This, the earliest system of true "superhighways" became a model for not only other states, but national and international projects as well. The concept and development of the Federal Interstate highway network and the German Autobahn can be traced as descendants of the Long Island parkway system.

Even as construction began on the Long Island parkways in the 1920s, the road system was noted for innovative design features and meticulous attention to aesthetics. The earliest parkways continued the tradition of continuous, curvilinear undivided parkways built earlier around New York. However, with the opening of the Meadowbrook State Parkway in 1934, the United States witnessed the first fully divided, limited access highway which would be the model for all subsequent Long Island parkway projects. As the years passed, the earliest roads, such as the Southern State Parkway, were rebuilt to the Meadowbrook model. However, as roads were upgraded, the original roadbed was rarely altered in this process. Rather, an identical set of traffic lanes and bridges was built adjacent to the earlier road thus separating traffic and doubling capacity. To this day only the careful observer on the Southern and Northern State Parkways in Nassau County will recognize that the two directions of the roads were built at different times, in the case of the Northern State literally decades later.

The one major deviation from Moses' original parkway plan

Southern State Parkway showing original lampost and overpass, 1937
Courtesy of Long Island State Parks Commission

was the rerouting of the Southern State Parkway through Hempstead Lake in the 1940s. The road, which originally skirted around the south edge of the lake, proved to be a bottleneck and serious traffic hazard. Moses wisely decided to eliminate the dog-leg turns and straighten the parkway in the interest of public safety.

While much has been written about the engineering features of Long Island's parkways and their importance to highway development in the world community, the simple beauty of the roads and their harmony with nature has often been overlooked. No detail in their construction was small enough to be overlooked by Robert Moses. He personally selected each and every element that would be visible to passing motorists. His statement that "Nothing is too good for the people of the Empire State" was certainly never truer than on Long Islands' parkways.

One of the most distinctive visual features of Long Island's parkways is the extensive used of ashlar granite, used to construct overpasses, gas stations and ancillary structures. Rarely are two overpasses alike, and, even when similar, subtle attempts to give each a separate identity are apparent. Stone quoins or arches may be set into the surface of a bridge. The Corona Avenue overpass in Valley Stream has a curved stone staircase with a wrought iron rail that descends to the parkway median below. Other bridges incorporated extensive landscaping which blossomed with dogwood, azalea and cascading English Ivy high above the Southern State.

The parkway gas stations, police and maintenance buildings similarly echoed the English countryside on Long Island. Buildings were, of course, constructed with random-coursed dressed granite and roofed in either slate or copper. Pergolas were commonly used to hide modern conveniences. The overall effect was to imitate the outbuildings of a typical Long Island estate.

Lighting the parkways was of no small concern to Moses, and various designs for iron light stantions submitted to him were rejected. Instead he instructed his engineers to design a lightpost made of wood which would echo the deciduous trees of the Long Island landscape. Ultimately the post that was selected was a hewned and chamfered design that included a tapered cross arm and decorative diagonal brace. Quaint iron lamps hung from the cross arm over the main parkway traffic lanes and exit ramp lights were more reminiscent of hanging lanterns. To sustain visual interest, single and double bracketed lampposts were alternated along the parkways between medians and roadsides. Over the years as parkway travel increased and roads were widened, the lighting fixtures became taller and larger. Still, the overall design imitated the original and the lights which updated the Northern State Parkway in its 1968 reconstruction were simply larger scale versions of their 1930 predecessors. (While several early parkway lamps remain forgotten along New York City's Belt Parkway in Brooklyn, only one remains in Nassau. It is located along Ocean Parkway, just west of the Jones Beach traffic circle.) As parkway construction spread westward into the New York City limits during the 1930s and 40s the wooden lampposts followed. However, due to the need for increased lighting in Brooklyn and Queens, certain overpasses there were lit by carefully designed cast iron lamps.

Signage on the parkways was also carefully integrated to impart the least visual intrusion on the surrounding landscape. In Nassau and Suffolk Counties, signs were framed in rusticated wood and painted black with capitalized white lettering. Within New York City limits, parkway signs were identical to their Long Island counterparts, except that they were white enamel with black lettering. The New York signs often were adorned with lighting hung on decorative iron brackets. The tops of both lampposts and sign posts were notched with decorative "lambs tongues," a simple but effective design decision that served to connect various road elements and evoke an overall parkway image of taste and refinement.

Fencing and rails along Long Island's parkways were also constructed of wood, much of it obtained from the Lloyd Neck area after the hurricane of 1938. The original specifications called for squared split railing set in posts with beveled tops. (Some examples of this very early fencing is still in place adjacent to the overpasses along the Wantagh State Parkway.) Over the years the rusticated rails gave way to a machine sawn design that allowed for their increased production as the parkways expanded and demand for fencing increased. However, the overall visual effect was virtually the same as the original.

Landscaping along the entire parkway route was lavished on

the system. Trees and shrubs indigenous to Long Island were planted under the guidance of Clarence Coombs, landscape architect. Whenever possible existing landscape features important to the site, such as nineteenth-century lopped trees in Huntington or the stately pines of the mile-long former August Belmont driveway in Babylon, were incorporated into the parkway design. The curvilinear road forms were specifically designed to heighten visual interest and enhance scenic vistas. An element of surprise lay beyond each parkway curve. Where necessary, eyesores beyond the parkway right of way were screened with plantings or latticework. When large scale construction projects caused inevitable disruption to parkway appearance, large signs apologized for the temporary disarray and assured passing motorists that the landscaping would be restored.

When the first Long Island parkways opened, they were an instant success. Not only did they increase recreational opportunities and expedite traffic in the region, they assured New Yorkers of the primacy of their state. The motoring public was awestruck at this unique public works effort which was unparalleled in American history. The parkways set the tone for a distinct quality of life on Long Island and at the same time made all parts of Nassau and Suffolk more easily accessible. Yet in many ways the parkways doomed the special qualities of Long Island that Robert Moses sought to enhance.

After World War II, drastic changes in Federal policies resulted in the explosion of suburban areas across the country. Urban housing constraints, coupled with subsidized veterans' mortgages resulted in continuous waves of development over sparsely settled urban fringes. In the New York region the effects of such policies were felt most intensely on Long Island. Inexpensive farmland was readily available for large scale development and the area lacked the underlying bedrock which often thwarted builders in Westchester County and Connecticut. More importantly, however, Long Island was already serviced by a parkway system unequalled in the New York area. Housing developments and commercial areas sprang up almost overnight adjacent to parkway exits.

Even the inevitable suburban development of Long Island did not have an impact on Moses' parkways at first. Anticipating that the land adjacent to state parkway right of ways might someday be developed, Moses wisely had restrictions in place authorizing review by the Long Island State Park Commission of all land development within 500 feet of a state park or parkway. For the most part, this resulted in a beautifully planned relationship between highway and residential development. The park strip along parkway right of ways bred other compatible uses such as schools, parks, playgrounds and public water facilities. Only through the determination of Robert Moses was commercial and industrial development prevented from seriously intruding upon the parkway system.

Over the half century of Robert Moses' association with Long Island's state parkways, a primary feature of their fame was a high standard of meticulous maintenance. Despite the massive changes to the Long Island landscape during the Moses reign of power, the appearance and feeling of driving on a state parkway changed very little over the years. Although by the 1950s the parkways' evolution as commuter roads was assured, the original design scheme of "parks for people in cars" was never compromised.

During the cost conscious 1970s, parkway jurisdiction passed from the Long Island State Park Commission to the New York State Department of Transportation. Soon after, large scale changes to the parkway design ethic began. In the interest of providing safer highways for higher speed traffic, while encouraging expanded use for larger vehicles and maximum carrying capacity, expressway-type highway elements have been promoted on the once rustic parkways. Present efforts seek to adhere to Federal highway standards developed for contemporary American superhighways, most of which allow high volume truck traffic. These standards are inevitably in conflict with the aesthetic principles developed years earlier for the Long Island roadways by Robert Moses. Visual and aesthetic considerations, once primary in state parkway policy, are now relegated to an incidental role in the bureaucratic planning process.

The changes to the Long Island parkway system since 1977 have resulted, to a large extent, in the "homogenization" of the parkway landscape and have encouraged major commercial and industrial land uses in previously restricted areas. The result is that Long Island's once magnificent parkways, among the most scenic and historic of America's roadways, now appear little different from most suburban interstates. While the parkways continue to serve Long Island as major transportation corridors, their significance as vehicular works of art remains largely a memory.

BIBLIOGRAPHY

Caro, Robert A. *The Power Broker: Robert Moses and the Fall of New York*. New York: Alfred A. Knopf, 1974.

Clarke, G. D. "The Parkway Idea," *The Highway and the Landscape*, ed. W. B. Snow. New Brunswick: Rutgers University Press, 1959.

Felleman, John P. and Thomas Nieman. "The Incorporation of Esthetics Within the Comprehensive Highway Development Process." C. P. L. Exchange Bibliography #1141, October, 1976.

Jackson, Kenneth T. "The Capital of Capitalism: The New York Metropolitan Region, 1890, 1940," *Metropolis, 1890, 1940* ed. Anthony Sutcliffe. Chicago: University of Chicago Press, 1984.

Labatut, Jean and Wheaton Lane, eds. *Highways in Our National Life*. New York: Arno Press, 1972.

Pushkarev, Boris and Christopher Tunnard. *Man-made America: Chaos or Control?* New Haven: Yale University Press, 1963.

Robinson, John. *Highways and Our Environment*. New York: McGraw-Hill, 1971.

United States Department of Transportation. *American Highways, 1876, 1976*. U.S. G.P.O. #050-001-00123-1. Washington, D.C., 1978.

Courtesy of Nassau County Museum Reference Library

West Bathhouse pool, Jones Beach

An Inside View of Jones Beach
Peter L. Kramer

Probably the most famous of Robert Moses' creations is Jones Beach State Park. Anyone who has studied the life and work of Robert Moses or the history of Long Island is familiar with the story of how Jones Beach came into being; not so familiar are the details of the inner workings of the Park. Since its creation, Jones Beach has been visited by almost half a billion people who have enjoyed its plantings, clean white sand, boardwalk, and ocean view. Recently the park has also been the site of Congressional hearings concerned with ocean dumping and the disposal of sewage and waste. (Interestingly, the hearing took place in the same building where "The Girl from Jones Beach," starring Ronald Reagan, was filmed in the 1940s.)

The park is many different things to many different groups of people. For the bird watchers there are areas of the park that afford incomparable opportunities to watch and study shore birds. Sport fishermen and surfcasters enjoy nothing more than spending a day at the West End of Jones Beach, while surfers call that same area of the Park one of the best surfing spots on the East Coast. Ocean bathing beckons on one side, and bay swimming at Zach's Bay on the other.

Armies of sunbathers have tanned and burned on the beach giving little thought to the hundreds of square dancers who drive from miles around to dance at the Bandshell on summer nights. Meanwhile, the roller skating rink is a source of pleasure to skaters who would prefer to be nowhere else.

Jones Beach is a magnificent miniature golf course to the more than 50,000 people who play each year on an eighteen-hole course designed and laid out by skilled park tradesmen. Each hole in the course recalls one of the State parks in the Long Island region: the Jones Beach hole features a water tower; a carousel, the symbol of Hempstead Lake State Park, adorns another; and a handmade wooden clubhouse, representing the world's largest public golfing facility at Bethpage State Park, dominates another part of the course. Both Hempstead Lake and Bethpage State Parks are Robert Moses creations, and, continuing his practice of attention to detail, all of the props for the miniature golf course were built by carpenters and staff persons at Jones Beach.

Jones Beach is a steaming bowl of clam chowder to the strollers who visit the Park on even the coldest and windiest days of the year. Jones Beach State Park never closes; it is open every day of the week and every week of the year. Indeed, the winter people welcome the end of summer, for when the crowds have gone the park becomes theirs.

Each summer, thousands of bathers use the salt water pool at the West Bathhouse and the fresh water pool at the East Bathhouse. The West Bathhouse pool was recently renovated and all of its electrical and plumbing systems modernized. The masonry work on the huge building was updated and repaired, but in such a way as to render the repairs all but invisible. Even the style of the original masonry has been retained so that the flavor of the architectural intent has not been compromised. The East Bathhouse pool complex is at present undergoing an equally meticulous renovation.

In the early 1980s when attendance at the Jones Beach Theatre waned, the State sought a new format for its presentations. Despite considerable skepticism, parks officials introduced a program of contemporary and rock music concerts. This was not an easily reached decision, for there were many who feared that such programs would bring unruly crowds to the Theatre who would damage the park's image. Working closely with community advisory groups and with the promoter retained by the State, the parks management formulated strict policy guidelines. In the Robert Moses tradition of maintaining the parks in the best possible condition while providing wholesome entertainment, the State decided to ban the service of alcoholic beverages at the Theatre. Though initially viewed as too restrictive, the policy is now generally accepted as having contributed to making the Jones Beach Theatre one of the safest and most enjoyable places to attend a concert.

While the change in policy has proven quite successful at the Theatre, other changes at the Park have not been so welcome. In

An Inside View of Jones Beach

Courtesy of Nassau County Museum Reference Library

West games area, Jones Beach

the 1960s, full-time and seasonal staff working at the height of the summer numbered twice that which presently staff the Jones Beach State Park complex. This reduction is even more severe than is immediately apparent, since Jones Beach is now considerably larger than it was in the 1960s. Then only one pool was in operation, and the West End of the park, consisting of two ocean front parking fields and the Jones Beach Marina, had not been constructed. Thus, the present day management of Jones Beach is forced to do more work with less staff, at a time when budget crunches and, more recently, a change in the demographics of Long Island's population have made it difficult to find and keep an adequate staff.

The same economic strictures have kept Jones Beach from further growth and expansion, even though the park was designed and built with expansion in mind. There are underpasses already in place, built decades ago so that unbuilt parking fields would be connected to unbuilt ocean front beaches, enabling park visitors to get from their cars to the beach without crossing the highway. An underground reservoir, built many years ago to meet possible future needs, is unused. The further expansion which would necessitate use of this reservoir has never occurred.

As it exists today, Jones Beach operates, in many respects, like a small city. In fact, on its busiest days, when more than 250,000 people present themselves at the gates, the population at the State Park is larger than that of most cities in this country. To satisfy their thirst, Jones Beach pumps its own fresh water from the aquifer nearly a thousand feet below the earth's surface. The water is pumped from three wells which refill the famed water tower; the tower, in turn, provides fresh water to the entire park. A water treatment plant purifies the sewage generated in the park each day. Road repair and garbage collection are performed by the park's own work crews. The park grows its own flowers, and the floral displays which so beautify the park walkways and promenades are changed on a rotating basis. Skilled tradesmen do the repair and maintenance work throughout the park.

The water treatment plant mentioned above was built in the 1950s, before the ocean dumping of sewage was an issue of public concern. The plant is still considered modern, and is equipped with the capability of generating its own electricity in the event of a power interruption. This precludes the possibility of Jones Beach having to release untreated sewage into the ocean in a power failure.

The park still has its own fire truck, one of the old fashioned kind seen now only in parades. Fortunately, the truck is not used any more, and the park makes use of the area fire departments. Jones Beach has an extensive emergency medical service consisting of well trained and well coordinated emergency medical technicians who are capable of treating scores of people every day, for injuries ranging from splinters and bug bites to cardiac emergencies and child birth. The New York State Park Police provide police service at Jones Beach and at all of the Long Island State Parks, as well as on the roadways between and within the parks. During the summer season the park police are one of the very busiest police agencies on Long Island, handling all sorts of police matters ranging from traffic accidents and violations to airplane crashes and the most serious kinds of emergencies.

Over the years it has become apparent that Jones Beach and its regular users are resistant to change. Even the most minor operational or aesthetic alteration in the park will draw close

Courtesy of Nassau County Museum Reference Library

Power boats in Zachs Bay, Jones Beach State Park, 1935.

scrutiny from the regular park visitors and the community groups comprising a local advisory committee. Regional parks officials welcome the input of the park-using public, and make great efforts to work with their constituency.

Indeed, when speaking with someone who has just visited Jones Beach after an absence of, perhaps, many years, it is interesting and pleasing to hear that the place looks much the way it did in the past. Standards of quality and cleanliness may be unequalled in any other public facility, yet the budgetary problems which have plagued the park for the past several years make it increasingly difficult to maintain these standards. The staff and money shortages which are now a part of the park's daily life must eventually take their toll. While park users and their elected representatives are quick to point out any housekeeping deficit which they observe, these same people are silent when the budget is being prepared in Albany. Thus the Jones Beach management, and management in all of Long Island's parks, is constantly pressed to do more work with diminished resources. This is unfortunate, because the programs and facilities will suffer from this strain, and, sooner or later, the public will begin to notice.

That which is not repaired today will eventually have to be replaced, and at a much higher cost.

If Robert Moses were to visit Jones Beach today, I imagine he would be pleased to see that his creation has survived the political, social, and economic changes which have marked the decades since its opening. He might be saddened to see some of the aesthetic changes, and the staffing problems might cause him to don a uniform and go to work. But if he heard the laughter of children playing on clean, white sand or splashing in the pool water, and saw strollers on the boardwalk everywhere around, I think he would know that his dream is still being realized.

Robert Moses as Hofstra Trustee, 1943–1956: Potent Preeminence to Petty Politics

Natalie A. Naylor

A decidedly lesser known side of Robert Moses' activities was his role as a trustee of Hofstra College (now Hofstra University). This aspect of his career is perhaps more important to Hofstra's history than to Moses' where it may be only a footnote. In 1958, two years after he had resigned from the Hofstra Board of Trustees, under circumstances to be described later, Robert Moses explained his view of his role at the time he became a trustee:

> They asked me to reorganize that college back in the early 1940s. At that time, the school was dead as a doornail. I got the thing on its feet. I picked Adams, persuaded him to come in.[1]

Is this an egotistical exaggeration? Perhaps, but not too far from the truth. Hofstra opened in 1935 as an extension of New York University, offering a two-year program. It soon became an independent four-year college, with a provisional charter in 1937 and an absolute charter in 1940. Prospects seemed bright until the Second World War intervened and enrollments dropped precipitously. Then the college's first president, Truesdel Calkins died of a heart attack in 1942. Since it was operating at a deficit, some of the trustees wanted to close the college for the war's duration. However, when Acting President Howard Brower consulted with the New York State Education Department, the Associate Commissioner for Higher Education recommended that the college remain open. He suggested increasing the number of trustees, recommending specifically that Robert Moses be asked to join the Board.[2]

At a special meeting of the Hofstra Board on December 24, 1943, Moses was elected trustee. At the very next meeting, he was appointed chair of the Post War Planning Committee and added to the committee already charged with the search for a new president.[3]

President John Cranford Adams

Moses played a significant role on both of these committees, especially the search committee. At the time he joined it, the college had been without a full-time president for eighteen months, so Moses sought recommendations for the post from among his numerous acquaintances. One of those suggested was John Cranford Adams, a Shakespeare scholar at Cornell University. Moses was one of three key trustees who interviewed Dr. Adams in New York City and, at a special meeting of the Board on June 28, 1944, the committee unanimously recommended he be offered a three year contract as president. Moses thus played a very significant role in bringing Adams to Hofstra, and his own later statement that he picked Adams and persuaded him to come has validity.[4]

John Cranford Adams was *the* decisive figure in shaping Hofstra's history over the next twenty years, but Moses played an important role, particularly in the early years, and continued to be a force to be reckoned with throughout his tenure as Hofstra trustee. Adams himself observed, in his later unpublished "Reflections of Hofstra," "Mr. Moses was not willing to chair the Board, but what he wanted he generally got."[5]

Adams recounts a "useful lesson" he learned from Moses during his first year as president. He had asked the trustees for $300 to repair the steps to Hofstra Hall, and $400 for new linoleum in the entrance hall:

> Mr. Moses cut short my explanations to propose a lump sum of $1000 for repairs as needed, adding "You may replace the linoleum with gorgonzola cheese if you see fit, but never again waste the time of your trustees with such trivial matters."[6]

Moses the Planner

In February 1944, Moses was appointed Chairman of the Post War Planning Committee for Hofstra. In its report to the full Board, the Committee identified Nassau, Suffolk, and eastern Queens as the prime areas for student recruitment. Limited dormitory facilities might be desirable, but fraternities and sororities were not favored. They recommended that the college should acquire additional land, should attempt to purchase a parcel of land west of the college, and negotiate for Mitchel Field "at the proper time." It was felt the "time was not ripe to discuss graduate work," and, though the Committee was divided on this, most felt that after the war, evening and extension couses should be discontinued.[7]

Planning disappears from the Trustee Minutes for nearly a year and a half; then, in October of 1945, Moses distributed to the trustees proposals for discussion by the Board. The ten point plan seems clearly to have been Moses' own vision for the future of Hofstra in the post-war years. Just as clearly, his vision was of an undergraduate commuter college serving local Long Island students.[8] The minutes are silent about the reactions of the other trustees to this plan, but President Adams later recalled:

> "Dormitories for Hofstra?" Bob Moses made it abundantly clear that so much as a mention of the word in a trustee meeeting would elicit his immediate resignation. To serve the local area had been the College's raison de'etre from the beginning. It still made sense, whereas trying with our meager resources to emulate Colegate or Amherst did not. Mr. Moses prevailed, even though several trustees did not share his views.[9]

One of the first of his ten points to be ignored was the ninth item, prohibiting honorary degrees. This was put aside when the trustees voted "that suitable honorary degrees be conferred upon Trustee Robert Moses and Trygve Lie at Commencement Exercises of June 1948." Was this a way of honoring Moses or of getting him to change his mind? Most likely both. Apparently Moses had not yet been approached on the matter, since at the next Executive Committee meeting, President Adams reported that Robert Moses "would accept an honorary degree (L.L.D.) from the College and would be present at Commencement to receive it."[10]

Potent Preeminence

Moses brought several new trustees to the enlarged Board which broadened its composition beyond Hempstead businessmen and local school superintendents. Alicia Patterson, Augustus

Weller, George Hauser, Eleanor Van Alen, and Charles E. Adams provided not only prestige, but important leadership.[11]

In November 1944, Moses was appointed to several committees (two of which he chaired) which were to solicit contributions from foundations and benefactors. He was one of three trustees appointed in December of that year "to investigate the financial condition of the college and suggest remedial action." From 1945 to 1950, Moses served as a "member-at-large" on the Executive Committee of the Board and on the Buildings and Grounds Committee. He took an active role in landscaping the campus and arranged for planned tree plantings.[12]

Moses very early asserted his dominant personality. Concerned about a possible conflict of interest when he realized that Board Chairman Brower[13] operated his lumber business on property leased from the Hofstra estate, Moses resorted to what had become, in other areas of operation, his favorite tactic. He threated to resign if Brower did not permit outside accountants to investigate his lumber company's financial records dating from the time the college had opened. Faced with this ultimatum, Brower agreed to the investigation.

Three accountants "known to Mr. Moses" carefully investigated and cleared Brower's name, concluding that, where there might have been any conflict, he had consisitently put the college's interests first. Brower, however, never attended another meeting. He resigned as chairman, later as college treasurer, and, finally, as trustee. Clearly, he was a victim of Robert Moses.[14]

President Adams and other trustees made many accommodations to Moses. Board by-laws specified that absence from three regular meetings was regarded as a form of resignation.[15] Although this provision was not always enforced, Moses was the *only* trustee allowed the privilege of sending a substitute, which some of the other trustees resented. Chester R. Blakelock, Executive Secretary of the Long Island Park Commission, represented and reported for Moses at most trustee and executive committee meetings. There were 49 regular meetings of the Hofstra trustees from December 1943, when Moses was elected to the Board, until May 1956, when his resignation was accepted. Moses himself attended only *two* of those meetings (in December 1944 and January 1945); Blakelock attended 29 of the 49 meetings as Moses' representative and was present at the two Moses attended. The pattern was similar for Executive Committee meetings; of 73 held, Moses attended 2 (in June and December 1945) and Blakelock 30.[16]

The efforts of Moses and other trustees to attract foundation support apparently were not successful in 1944, and it is probably significant that the two regular meetings Moses did attend focused on the financial condition of the college. He personally submitted the committee's report for a two year financial program and a slate of new officers for the Board, following Brower's resignation. Moreover, Blakelock certainly kept Moses well informed. In his memoirs, Adams noted, "if Mr. Moses came less regularly to Board meetings, he at least sent an observer, and when some line of action displeased him, Mr. Hauser [Chairman of the Trustees] or I was sure to hear his views the next morning."[17]

Probably one of the most significant contributions of Robert Moses to Hofstra was in the area of physical expansion of the institution. The Post War Planning Committee had recommended that the College acquire additional land. Small parcels were purchased when they became available, but the campus area more than doubled in 1947 with the acquisition of 35 acres east of the campus. Adams recalled, "With board approval, prompted by Trustee Moses, we wrote several times to the owner." President Adams and Trustee Augustus Weller negotiated the purchase and agreed on a price of $70,000. Adams continued, "the Bursar went white to lips when informed of a commitment of this magnitude at a time when College finances were only just out of the red, but the Trustees—especially Hauser, Moses, and Weller—never hesitated."[18]

Moses thus played an important role in enabling Hofstra to physically expand its campus which, ironically, enabled it to grow into a larger institution than he had envisioned. However, in 1954, Moses did stifle discussion for a Suffolk branch, which had been mentioned in the newspapers. The Minutes record, "Speaking for Trustee Moses, Mr. Blakelock suggested that the College should drop the project and release this fact to the press." Each member was polled and a motion passed that the college was "not now in a position to expand to another campus."[19]

Moses played a role also in Aymar Embury becoming the college architect. Embury had designed the original buildings on the quadrangle in the New York University years, but was reluctant to do additional buildings because of changes that had been made in his plans. President Adams reports that Embury had a "change of heart" when he heard that Moses was a Hofstra trustee.[20] The results of this change can be seen in the well designed architecture of the Hofstra campus.

By the 1950s, Moses was less of a presence as a Hofstra Trustee. President Adams was now firmly in control of the college which was on a sound financial basis and moving in new directions. Moses did not approve of some of these directions, such as offering graduate degrees and discussing dormitories. In fact, he apparently threatened again to resign, since the Minutes report in April 1955, "Trustee Moses has assured President Adams that he would not resign from the Board if Mr. Blakelock were elected to membership." The Board acceeded to this request and Blakelock joined the Board as a trustee.[21]

Moses organized a regional planning forum held at Hofstra in September 1955. Twenty invited speakers addressed various aspects of population and industrial growth, health and welfare, school needs, transportation and recreation, and future planning, focusing on Nassau County which was then the fastest growing county in the country.[22]

In November 1955, Robert Moses sent the Board one of his rare communications, which was presented at a meeting that neither Moses nor Blakelock attended. The Minutes report:

> Following lengthy discussion it was felt that the College should not openly press for the relocation of Mitchel Field, but should actively seek the help of those who might aid us in acquiring at least 100 acres across Fulton Avenue fronting the campus when land became available.[23]

Significantly, the trustees decided not to seek the aid of Robert Moses in this, but rather that of Trustee Leon Swirbul, President of Grumman Aircraft, and, through Trustee Alicia Patterson, of realtor and developer William Zeckendorf. Apparently, Moses was upset that Hofstra did not agree with his proposal (which may have involved an exchange of land), but the exact nature of the proposal is unclear.

Resignation

A year later, in March 1956, Moses resigned and this time he refused to rescind his decision. The parting came when Moses objected to three Hofstra faculty members supporting the Democratic planning bill for Nassau County. Moses had called this plan unworkable and a "totalitarian communistic concept." In turn, one of the Hofstra faculty referred to Moses' irresponsible name-calling" in a letter to the editor in *Newsday*. Moses attached this clipping to his letter of resignation, explaining:

> I am not going to waste further time protesting the use of Hofstra College in the presentation of extreme views on Charter and planning matters. This subject was approached in a dignified way at the Forum at Hofstra. Every citizen, of course, has a right to express his views but he has no right to use the name and influence of a conservative private college if he is a member of the faculty.
>
> Personally, I don't care to be accused of "deliberate misrepresentation" and a "bald attempt to deceive the people" by an inexperienced junior member of the faculty who so far as I know has never himself accomplished anything in this field.[24]

President Adams wrote Moses, "I am profoundly distressed that any member of the Hofstra faculty should cause you annoyance." He indicated that the Provost had advised the faculty that they should be careful "to distinguish their rights as citizens and obligations as members of a college faculty."[25] Adams concluded by saying he hoped that Moses would "reconsider" his resignation "that would cause lasting regret" to his "many friends on this campus." Moses' response was blunt: "Thanks for your letter. I'm out. Too much annoyance!"[26]

Moses later revealed that following his resignation the trustees sent a committee to see him, and, in fact, Chairman Weed, Trustee Weller, and President Adams did visit, but were unable to convince Moses to reconsider. "They got very apologetic," he claimed, adding, "I didn't want to be connected with the college—I had many other jobs to do ... My reputation doesn't depend on Hofstra College."[27]

Epilogue

No reasons were stated publicly at the time of Moses' resignation, but the story does not end here. More than two years after his resignation, Robert Moses wrote to architect Aymar Embury:

> You spoke to me about Hofstra the other day. I got off the Board of Trustees although I was still interested in the institution (having done something to put it on its feet and to recruit John Cranford Adams) partly because of the pressure of work and partly because I was disgusted with the use of the college name by faculty people who mess into public affairs of which they are completely ignorant.[28]

This last sentence was released to the press (in the midst of local election campaigns) by J. Russel Sprague, Nassau County Republican leader, to whom Moses had sent a copy. Moses mentioned specifically a proposal for a railroad spur to Jones Beach proposed by Hofstra Economics Professor Charles Stonier, which, together with Stonier's opposition to Moses' Verrazano Bridge project, may have occasioned the outburst. Both of these proposals, however, were in 1958, long after Moses had left the Hofstra Board of Trustees. Sprague, in his statement, referred to Hofstra professors supporting the Democratic planning bill, advocating a county-wide sales tax for schools, and being involved with a Democratic political poll. He urged the Hofstra Trustees to "look into this constant sniping and pettifoggery by pedagogues who are peddling a straight party line packaged in a Hofstra label."[29] In the 1950s, of course, that phrase, "straight party line," was an allusion to the Communist party.

Now the Moses-Hofstra split was in all the newspapers, *Newsday*, the *Long Island Press*, and the *New York Times*. When *Newsday* called Moses for a statement on Sprague's release and asked if he had resigned because of political activities by faculty, Moses said: "That was one of my chief reasons, although there were other considerations. They were not only dabbling in politics. They were making personal attacks on me." He went on to make the statements quoted above about having been asked to reorganize the college and bringing in Adams as president. He added, "Adams has always been interested in making a big university out of Hofstra. He wants to build dormitories. I disagree. I think it should be a local college . . . He had grandiose ambitions. I was against it and I said so. That was one of the other reasons." Continuing his *ad hominum* charges, he added, "And while they're attacking us, Adams is licking our boots trying to get land for use as an athletic field at one-quarter its value."[30]

The day following Sprague's news release, one of the professors sent President Adams a two-page memo of comments on the activities Sprague mentioned, concluding:

> In every case I think it clear the faculty people are completely innocent of the charge that they used the name of Hofstra to advance the welfare of the Democratic party. The activities in which they engaged were in every case a result of their professional competence, a competence which the Democrats have demonstrated a willingness to employ but which the Republicans have chosen to ignore.[31]

Newsday also ran an editorial, "The Right to Disagree: A Shameful Effort to Strangle Academic Freedom" and this set the tone for the response. It became an issue of academic freedom: the right of professors to speak on political issues. The *Newsday* editorial noted that Moses "is apparently willing to damage the reputation of a fine college and to collaborate in an attempt to muzzle academic freedom. It is a sad footnote to the life of a notable public servant."[32]

John Cranford Adams came out of the fray as a defender of academic freedom. His "Academic Freedom" file is filled with letters of congratulation for his stand from other college presidents, educational leaders, and interested citizens. Editors of the student newpaper headlined their editorials "Gutter Politics" and "A Job Well Done."[33]

There are two footnotes to this account of Robert Moses and Hofstra. First, when Hofstra did secure a large section of Mitchel Field in 1962, President Adams sent Moses a letter thanking him for his assistance. Moses responded, "I was delighted to help, and if I added anything, am amply compensated. My chums all feel the same way."[34] The "help" had evidently come in the form of a recommendation, for Moses had headed a planning committee appointed by County Executive A. Holly Patterson on the future of Mitchel Field, and that committee, along with Mr. Patterson and *Newsday*, supported the allocation of substantial portions of Mitchel Field for Hofstra and Nassau Community College.

The second footnote is that Adams' successor, Clifford Lord, sought Moses' advice and later his help to obtain additional Mitchel Field land. (The Hofstra *Chronicle* reported, "Moses Seeks More Land for Lord.") Hofstra received an additional 67 acres in 1967, and Robert Moses was named an Honorary Trustee.[35]

Conclusion

When Moses joined the Hofstra Board of Trustees, he was a potent force—the only member who was well known beyond local circles. It was definitely a "feather in Hofstra's cap" to have a trustee of the stature of Moses, but he was a very intimidating figure.[36] Especially in the early years, Moses' dominant personality resulted in a behavior of deference on the part of President Adams and the other trustees.[37] President Adams himself was a strong personality, however, and it was inevitable that the two would eventually clash. Moses did not get what he wanted and finally resigned, after several threats to do so, despite the efforts of Adams and other trustees to appease him. The quiet resignation of Moses in 1956 had led to the adoption of a policy on faculty statements, so when the reasons became public in 1958, in the form of petty political accusations, President Adams could turn it into a defense of academic freedom.

Unfortunately, Moses' resignation was a blot on his genuine accomplishments as Hofstra trustee. John Cranford Adams later acknowledged the contributions of Robert Moses: "He kept this college going. He appointed these four or five trustees who were the backbone of its administration for years. He befriended us in a hundred and one different ways."[38] An article in the *Saturday Evening Post* in 1960 provided an outsider's assessment:

> Mr. Moses has long since departed from the board, leaving some mildly bruised feelings in his wake, but the school still bears the stamp of his personality and his ideas. It was he who beat the academic bushes to find Doctor Adams.... It was also Mr. Moses who insisted that the school remain a community college, serving its own region and ignoring those students who might wish to come from Timbuctoo or Texas. Hofstra, he felt, was to be the urban college of the future and the urban community needed a school to which students could drive by car.[39]

Robert Moses' vision of the future of the college as a local, undergraduate, commuter college ultimately clashed with that of John Cranford Adams' and with the changing realities of American higher education in the 1950s.[40] With the establishment of its neighbor, Nassau Community College, Hofstra necessarily changed its focus. This does not diminish the fact, however, that Robert Moses played a crucial role in rescuing the college in 1944, and in planning for its future. Although it is now an institution following policies very different from those he proposed, the physical expansion of the campus, which he advocated and encouraged, made possible the development of today's Hofstra University.

NOTES

1. Quoted in *Newsday*, September 26, 1958.
2. John Cranford Adams, "Reflections of Hofstra," (hereafter, "Reflections") typescript, p. 11; "Minute Book," Board of Trustees, Hofstra College (hereafter cited as Minutes), November 18, 1943, p. 125A. (The bound volumes of Minutes and all other materials cited are in the University Archives in the Hofstra Library, unless otherwise indicated.) See also Clifford Lord, *The Hofstra Story* (Hempstead, NY: Hofstra University, 1972), pp. 5–8.
3. Minutes, December 24, 1943, p. 128 and February 25, 1944, p. 133.
4. Gilmore D. Clarke, Dean of College of Architecture, Cornell University to Moses, May 15, 1944, Robert Moses Papers, Rare Books and Manuscripts Division, The New York Public Library, Astor, Lenox and Tilden Foundations (hereafter cited as NYPL; microfilm copies of NYPL's Moses Papers related to Hofstra are in the Hofstra Archives). The State Education Department had a May 15 deadline on provisional registration of Hofstra programs, pending appointment of a full-time president. Moses successfully intervened with state officials for an extension to September 15, 1944. See Moses to William Wallin, Vice Chancellor, Regents, March 20, 1944, and his correspondence with Regent W. Kingsland Macy, April 24, 1944, May 1, 1944, and May 8, 1944, NYPL.
5. Adams, "Reflections," p. 11; see also Adams, oral history interview (hereafter. cited as interview), recorded June 8, 1978.
6. Adams, "Reflections," p. 50.
7. Minutes, May 12, 1944, pp. 137–138.
8. "Policies Suggested for Discussion by the Board by Robert Moses, October 20, 1945: (1) That it is the policy of the Board that the

College be a local institution serving Long Island east of the New York City line with the possible addition of the easterly section of the Borough of Queens; (2) That in the first instance only students from this area will be admitted; (3) That no effort be made to obtain students from other areas; (4) That Hofstra College shall serve day students only; (5) That Hofstra shall be strictly a College and not a University; (6) That Hofstra shall not be a residential college with residential fraternity or sorority houses and that it shall have no dormitories until such time that it proves beyond a doubt that they are absolutely essential to the operation of the college; (7) That Hofstra shall not have a graduate school or a summer school; (8) That courses shall be limited to Liberal Arts, Secretarial, Engineering and Home Economics; (9) That no Honorary Degrees be granted; (10) That no degrees be granted beyond degrees of Bachelor" (Minutes, October 25, 1945, p. 207).

9. Adams, "Reflections," p. 11; see also Adams, interview.

10. U. N. Secretary Trygve Lie apparently was unable to attend the 1948 commencement. The trustees later asked Moses to invite Lie to make the 1949 Commencement Address and receive an honorary degree. Lie accepted the invitation "in view of the importance" Moses attached to it and Moses read the presentation. Adams, "Reflections," p. 83; Minutes: March 17, 1948, p. 369; April 27, 1948, p. 376; December 15, 1948, p. 431; May 25, 1949, p. 490; and Lie to Moses, December 23, 1948, NYPL.

11. Adams, interview. Alicia Patterson was Editor of *Newsday;* Augustus Weller, President of Meadowbrook National Bank; George Hauser, a Vice President of Liberty Aircraft in Farmingdale; Mrs. James H. Van Alen (later, Mrs. Walter D. Fletcher), a locally prominent social and civic leader; and Charles E. Adams an engineer with the Long Island Rail Road. In his correspondence, Moses refers to his friends joining the board; see, for example, Moses to R. Fosdick, November 24, 1944, NYPL.

12. Minutes, December 14, 1944, p. 160; Hofstra Trustees Book, President's files, I: 43; Report of Special Committee to Investigate Finances, December 16, 1944, in Moses' Papers, NYPL. Moses reported proposals for operations and staff in 1945–46 and 1946–47; and presented the slate of trustees officers for 1945 (Minutes, January 18, 1945, p. 163, 165).

13. Brower, President of the Brower Lumber Corporation, had been a business associate of William Hofstra and an executor of the Hofstra estate, as well as Acting President of Hofstra for over two years.

14. Adams, "Reflections," pp. 51–52; Adams, interview; and "Report on 5 Years of Operations at June 30, 1944" in Moses' papers, NYPL.

15. Minutes, October 20, 1954, pp. 1322–1323.

16. Figures from Trustees' "Attendance" book.
17. Adams, "Reflections," p. 61. Some of Blakelock's memos to Moses reporting on the trustee meeting are in the Moses papers in NYPL.
18. Adams, "Reflections," p. 62.
19. Minutes, January 26, 1954. See also Moses' letter to Hauser (January 6, 1954, NYPL) objecting to Suffolk branch with copies to other trustees and responses to Moses from Leroy Weed (January 15, 1954), Alicia Patterson (January 18, 1954), and W. H. Vanderpoel (January 12, 1954), NYPL.
20. Adams, "Reflections," pp. 65–66.
21. Minutes, April 20, 1955, p. 1432 and October 19, 1955. Months before, Moses had written Adams, "I would like to see Chester Blakelock elected to the Board of Trustees and not merely as my representative" (October 22, 1954, NYPL). Adams supported this request. See Adams to Moses, October 25, 1954 and Moses to Adams, October 27, 1954, NYPL. Discussion of dormitories in Minutes, May 18, 1955, p. 1451.
22. The Executive Committee of the Trustees had "heartily concurred" when Moses suggested the forum and has resolved "that Moses be given all possible help by the College in the running of such a forum" (Minutes, June 29, 1955, pp. 1476–1477). Hofstra published the proceedings, *The Problems of Growth in Nassau and Western Suffolk* (1955). See also Adams to Moses, September 14, 1955; and Moses to Adams, September 17, 1955 and November 9, 1955, NYPL.
23. Minutes, November 10, 1955, p. 1537. (The letter from Moses could not be located.)
24. Moses to Leroy J. Weed, March 9, 1956, NYPL. The three Hofstra professors were Alan K. Campbell, Political Science, William Leonard in Economics, and Daniel Fusfield, Economics. Fusfield's letter appeared in *Newsday,* March 8, 1956. Leonard later discussed this incident in a long letter criticizing Moses in the *Long Island Daily Review,* March 3, 1959 (copy in Moses Honorary Degree file, Hofstra Archives).
25. The administration initially cautioned the faculty not to indicate their affiliation with Hofstra when speaking or writing as citizens. By January 1957, the College Faculty Executive Committee adopted a clarifying "Policy Regarding Public Utterances—Letters to the Editor," which stated that while faculty could give their affiliation, they should clarify that they were not speaking for the college. The Policy on Letters to the Editor is in Adams' correspondence, Academic Freedom file, and printed in the *Hofstra Chronicle* (student newspaper), October 1, 1958 and excerpted in *Newsday,* September 26, 1958.
26. Adams to Moses, March 13, 1956 and Moses to Adams, March 14, 1956, NYPL. Moses wrote fellow trustee Weller, "my mind is made up" (March 14, 1956, NYPL).

27. Minutes, April 12, 1956, p. 1618; Moses quoted in *Newsday*, September 26, 1958, p. 94. Blakelock also resigned; Minutes, May 9, 1956, p. 1618. See also the Academic Freedom file in Adams' correspondence.

28. Moses to Embury, September 15, 1958, NYPL.

29. "Why Moses Quit Hofstra College Out in Letter," n.d. [September 24, 1958], copy of Sprague's press release in Academic Freedom file, Adams correspondence.

30. *Newsday*, September 26, 1958. See also *Newsday*, September 25, 1958; *New York Times*, September 25 and 26, 1958; *Long Island Daily Press*, September 26, 1958; and *Hofstra Chronicle*, October 1, 1958. In the spring of 1958, Adams sought from Moses 30 acres of excess park land at the northwest intersection of Hempstead Turnpike and Meadowbrook Parkway. Moses was ready to sell and the Hofstra Board approved, but it was never finalized, perhaps because of "avigation rights" restrictions on the property. See Adams to Moses, April 18, 1958 and Moses to Adams, May 6, 1958, Adams correspondence, Mitchel Field folder.

31. Alan K. Campbell to Adams, September 26, 1958, Adams correspondence, Academic Freedom file.

32. *Newsday*, September 26, 1958. Apparently Moses tried to pressure Adams to fire the faculty members directly involved. Adams had dinner with Alicia Patterson, Editor of *Newsday*, the same day he received a copy of the news release and she assured him of *Newsday*'s support. See Adams, interview.

33. *Hofstra Chronicle*, October 1, 1958.

34. Moses to Adams, November 10, 1962, in Adams correspondence, Mitchel File folder. Adams sent the same letter to many others who had helped secure the Mitchel Field land.

35. Lord to Moses, June 25, 1964 and December 4, 1967, Moses Honorary Degree file; *Hofstra Chronicle*, December 1, 1966.

36. Caroline Dickie, Hartwick, N.Y., telephone interview, April 18, 1988. Miss Dickie was secretary to President Adams and the trustees beginning in 1946; she retired in 1963.

37. Adams, interview. On Moses' personality, see also William D. Ogden, "Striking a Balance on Robert Moses," *New York Times Magazine*, July 15, 1956, p. 14ff.

38. Adams, interview. See also Adams to Moses, June 10, 1964, Moses Honorary Degree file.

39. Harold H. Martin, "How to Start a College From Scratch," *Saturday Evening Post*, May 7, 1960, p. 59.

40. Moses later admitted, "I have come around reluctantly to the new Hofstra with all the trimmings of an expanding university . . . . I realize now in retrospect that I have been too nostalgic and unrealistic" (Robert Moses, "The Dilemma of Private Colleges," *Newsday*, July 20, 1968).

THE MOSES DESIGN

West Bathhouse at Jones Beach in the 1950s when the elegant wooden awning supports still stood on the upper deck

The Rustic and the Sophisticated in Park Design: The Moses Style vs the CCC

Frank B. Burggraf and Karen Rollet

When people visit a park they rarely give a thought to the style of its design. Indeed, for the most part park designers endeavor to work their craft in such a way as to draw as little attention to their creations as possible. There are, however, two discernible traditions of park design, one essentially derived from the Civilian Conservation Corps (CCC) and the other almost singlehandedly created by Robert Moses. A comparison of these styles can be made by examining the park design accomplished under Robert Moses, best exemplified by Jones Beach State Park, and the design and detailing accomplished by the CCC in demonstration areas, state, and national parks throughout the United States.

The park developments of the CCC were the result of the New Deal depression era relief programs. These programs were cooperative, with the federal government providing leadership, funding, and some design assistance, and the states providing manpower, design, and implementation. During this relatively short period of activity state park acreage alone increased by 67%. Increased comprehensive planning for state park development was another positive result of the CCC activity.

The organization of the CCC camps and their local situations had much to do with the type of facilities constructed. Often these facilities were a perfect example of the regional or local style expressed at its most rustic level. The traditional basic house or cabin design influenced the design of shelters, cabins, and administrative or concession buildings. Local materials, natural stone, and timber were almost always used.

It appears that at the time, the 1930s, the rustic conception was well accepted throughout the U.S. as being the appropriate expression of park facilities. The prototypes may have been the structure already built in the National Parks and those private retreats built in the Adirondacks. It must be remembered that there were no clients for the parks being created. Few people had the means and leisure to enjoy them, and those who did had little inclination to travel to remote parts of the country to recreate, except to such extraordinary areas as Yellowstone or Yosemite. These projects were built to keep men employed and coincidentally to train young men in craft skills.

Park visitors, those people who might travel to Yellowstone or arrange a guided hunting trip to the North woods, were few in number and were persons of means. It was logical, therefore, to create parks that were furnished in the manner such park users might expect to find when they left the cities to "rough it." There was a strong emphasis on scenic or wilderness conservation and passive recreation. The goal was to conserve the site in its natural state; facilities for recreational use were provided, but were subordinated to the protection and preservation of natural resources. In many instances depleted farms were planted with trees and streams were damned to create ponds which would provide little benefit to park users for many years.

The introductory statement in one of the publications of the National Park Service during this period is illuminating: "If man could bring to his creation in natural parks the protective coloration that Nature bestows on wildlife, with how much more harmony he would endow his trespasses!"[1]

Yet another factor contributing to the rustic design style was the personnel involved in the CCC program. The CCC Relief and Reforestation Act of 1933 employed single men between the ages of 18 and 25 with dependent relatives. The enrollees went to work for a particular agency, either the Department of Interior or Agriculture, or a state agency. Though a good number of the men were illiterate, they brought with them rudimentary skills typical of rural areas, carpentry, simple construction, etc. They also had a tradition of craft which came out of the necessity of satisfying living requirements with limited resources.

Some people, more highly educated and trained, worked with the Works Progress Administration. Adult men and women were hired to work on diverse public projects, among them parks. In this way, a few trained architects and landscape architects

The Rustic and the Sophisticated in Park Design 193

Sign handcarved and painted by the CCC, Arkansas

became part of the process of park development. The quality of design could sometimes be good, but construction methods had to be extremely simple since labor from the CCC camps was inexperienced. A check on the design quality was provided by submitting plans to the federal authorities. Sometimes young professionals supervised the work in the field, often designing as they went.

The nature of the work led to a recognizable style of design which verged on the vernacular. The rustic quality of natural materials with simple direct construction methods predominated. Because the process was labor intensive, individual craftsmanship and handwork became the dominant design expression. Poverty often determined project location, thus parks frequently were located in remote and rural areas with little expectation that they might ever attract large numbers of visitors or serve area population centers. Certainly the prospect of the common man in command of his own private conveyance was not the basis of design.

During this same period Robert Moses offered a vision of parks and recreation facilities that was unique and comprehensive. His vision of public recreation, while embracing natural beauty, was a broader and more inclusive one than that being assembled by the CCC. He saw the need to furnish the opportunity for a full range of active recreational pursuits and not just passive enjoyment of nature. He also had clients by the thousands, those people living in the inner city who needed recreation in full measure.

* * *

> ... after nearly a century of agitation for the creation of 'breathing spaces' in slums (Moses' grandfather, Bernhard Cohen, had been one of the agitators during the 1870s), there were on the Lower East Side—in an area a mile wide into which were crammed more than half a million people—exactly two small parks, neither of which contained a single piece of play equipment.[2]

The artist needs an informed and demanding client in order to produce his best work. For this reason the Medici were important to Michelangelo's great achievements, and for the same reason Robert Moses can be said to have been the Medici of parks. Well educated and traveled, he had very strong ideas about how he wanted his parks furnished. He had at his disposal experienced professionals, architects, engineers, and landscape architects, but he always participated in the detailed decision making process. For example, he insisted that benches were to sit on and therefore must have backs. He would not tolerate benches which many designers favored for their simplicity but which had no backs.

The shore at Jones Beach clearly represented an opportunity for swimming, but Moses' conception went far beyond a simple bathing beach. Moses directed the construction of a swimming pool and provided many forms of active recreation such as shuffleboard and paddle tennis. Stone was employed in the

The Rustic and the Sophisticated in Park Design

Example of signage at Jones Beach State Park

construction of buildings and bridges but it was not the coarse irregular masonry of the rustic style. Stone used at Jones Beach was not local. It was often ashlar, and carefully shaped and coursed. Life preservers, flags, fountains and other details added visual delight. The characteristics of an ocean cruise ship are manifested in the details of the bath house at Jones Beach. It is said that Moses wanted people to feel that they were really on a vacation—an ocean cruise—when they came to Jones Beach.

While the CCC projects were most often designed in the field with the workers themselves making decisions about the final product, those projects done under the direction of Robert Moses were executed in the office. Complete, detailed drawings were prepared, reviewed, and established the quality of the work. Skilled, experienced workers were more commonly available for the execution of the work than could be found in remote, rural CCC sites. Quality materials were employed. The bath house at

Jones Beach, for example, was built with quality materials and carefully developed detail. Swimming pools were tiled and lifeguard stands fabricated out of permanent, corrosion resistant metal not fabricated out of two by fours or pealed logs as they might be at a CCC camp site.

The highly refined design detailing was extended to include mundane utility structures, signs, curbs and gutters, waste receptacles, paving, etc. The nautical theme expressed at Jones Beach in such details results in much visual delight. Mosaic tile, bronze, marble and cut limestone are materials, never before associated with park design, that were used in plans influenced by Robert Moses. The guidelines and designs formulated by the National Park Service stressed rustic quality and practicality which came to characterize the CCC and WPA parks as a whole.

The 1938 publication called *Park and Recreation Structures* provided documentation of successful project designs as well as an explanation of the general philosophy underlying the rustic style of park architecture. Constant references were made to the importance of designing with "Nature." This point of view was firmly and consistently applied to structures as diverse as guard rails, retaining walls, comfort stations, bridges, cabins, shelters and even the lowly hand pump.

In studying the publication in detail, several general rules become apparent. One is the use of indigenous materials. In the northern woods of Minnesota, Michigan and Wisconsin, log structures were the rule. Where mature woods existed it was considered undesirable to cut too many trees, so fallen trees were sometimes salvaged, or logs were hauled in for construction. In the southwest, Texas, and the Rockies, stone structures predominated. In the east, wood structures were built, but they often used more refined finishes such as hand axed or adzed beams and planks. In Oklahoma and Arkansas, a combination of stone and logs testified to the availability of both materials.

In addition to the use of local materials, the design objective was to blend facilities into the site. The following statement offers an example: "one of the difficult park problems is the blending of a masonry barrier of retaining wall to a rock outcrop which it surmounts or abuts. The result in general seems to indicate failure to sense that skillful blending of the manmade to the natural was

The Rustic and the Sophisticated in Park Design 197

Rustic CCC style in Petit Jean State Park, Arkansas,
with splayed walls and heavy beams expressing solidity
and mass in nature

the essence of the problem, or else that skill was lacking. When the transition is so handled that the precise limits of Nature's handiwork and man's blur to the eye's satisfaction, the accomplishment is praiseworthy."[3]

A particularly good example of the application of this principle is found in a bathhouse and shelter structure at Crowley's Ridge State Park in Arkansas. The structure uses stone and wood, typical of the area. The lower level is built back into the hill, and is surrounded by battered or buttressed stone, splayed out to meet the ground. The method creates "assimilation into the site to a degree not attained by other approaches."[4] Also, the scale of the walls is oversized. The use of bold masonry and large timber members creates a scale deemed appropriate to rugged outdoors areas. The "heroic scale" becomes even more apparent in park structures in places such as Glacier National Park and other western national parks. The upper level of the structure at Crowley's Ridge is created of logs which range in size from 8" to 2' diameter. The quality of the design is found in the double and triple rhythm of the supports, the bracing of the joints, the three bays, and a railing design which mirrors all the other elements.

In addition to the concept of scale and using local materials, the National Park Service publication recommends the use of vernacular styles. For example, the traditional Adirondack shelter with an open porch and rough siding is transformed into a cabin design for Finger Lakes State Park. The southern "dogtrot," an open passage through the center of the house, turns up in a cabin in Weoqufka State Park, Alabama. The "Ramada," a covered shelter of the southwest derived from the Pueblo Indians is found in a picnic shelter in Mt. Metro Park in Phoenix. A one room cabin in Palo Duro State Park in Texas is a form typical of early adobe structures.

In its own modest way, the publication also grapples with the tenets of the modern movement which decreed honesty in materials, particularly manufactured materials and concrete. The use of unadorned concrete was considered a bad idea, even though it had the virtue of solidity. Concrete bridges are described thus: "there are far too many bridges which, after having broken every commandment for beauty and fitness, seem to have sought to wash away all sins through the virtue of permanence."[5]

A humorous discussion follows about the merits of hiding or disguising such mundane items as hand pumps, pumphouses and water towers. Hollowed out logs, shelters, stones, etc., cover up the hand pump, since this "neglected ugly duckling so challenges the chivalry of designers of park facilities that they ride forth in shining armor to see justice done."[6] At the same time, the park designer is cautioned from going too far in glorification of these items.

The design of CCC park structures was based on a philosophy of blending in with "Nature," and finding ways to use indigenous materials and styles of construction. The structures were not, however, built with large numbers of people in mind. They accommodated small groups, but never could have accommodated the thousands of people for whom Moses planned. The merits of CCC parks were hit and miss: if the ingredients came together with a sense of proportion and craftsmanship, the result was good, but sometimes the ingredients were ill fitting, ungainly, or contrived, and the result was bad. The system never had the quality control that Moses exercised in his park development.

Both the CCC parks and the parks supervised by Moses

Hodgepodge of styles, rustic and modern, showing lack of design and good materials at Hamanasett State Park, Arkansas

served the public, but each had a very different concept of what the public was likely to need or want. By and large, CCC work was conservation work, and its goals were to serve an anonymous public in presumably small numbers. The facilities themselves were one step away from being in a natural state. Each park was planned to have enough structures to accommodate proposed modest recreational uses of the area without diminishing the natural or scenic qualities of the park. Roads, trails and structures were planned as a functionally and aesthetically related group. Structures were to be of a scale compatible with the landscape and built from materials native to the area.[7]

Robert Moses envisioned a different sort of park. Not only did Moses insist on quality but on quantity. The scale of park facilities and parkways that were developed under his direction were extensive and comprise a system to which none are comparable. On the other hand, the demand for recreation opportunities was already well established. Robert Caro in the *Power Broker* reports that the attendance in 1921 at the Palisades Interstate Park was 3,100,000 and that in 1922 it topped four million.[8] For most of the parks constructed by the CCC there was no established visitor demand. The most visited national park today is the Blue Ridge Parkway which was similarly constructed during the depression years. At the time it was begun it was seen only as a means of providing employment in an area of desperate need; there was little or no prospect of tourist travel to warrant such a facility. No one foresaw (as Robert Moses did, working in another area) the greatly expanded ownership of private automobiles and leisure time that would permit millions to visit the parks created by such make-work projects.

Without the prospect of users or an estimate of the numbers to be served, the facilities were constructed in terms of what the sites seemed to suggest as appropriate. For the most part, the parks built during the 1930s served well into the 1950s before becoming taxed by overuse and age. Mission 66 was conceived as a ten-year building program by the National Park Service to upgrade and expand those facilities, many of which were originally built during the depression.

The slowdown in park construction marks another contrast between the CCC efforts and the Moses program, for Robert Moses was still initiating projects in the 1950s that expanded or added to the extraordinary system already in place. World War II ended the CCC program.

Not all states have accepted the role of providing recreation facilities and services for their citizens. Until the late 1950s, for example, the neighboring State of New Jersey had not expended any funds for acquisition of park land and possessed not a single mile of shoreline for public beach. Island Beach State Park came into being in 1958 through the Coast Guard decision that it no longer needed a lighthouse and the associated beach frontage. Acreage donated for recreational development went unused. Obviously New Jersey did not have a Robert Moses.

These two park design traditions, rustic and sophisticated, became the basis for design in parks across the country. The CCC tradition was already established, inspired by cabins built in the mountains of the Adirondacks and elsewhere, but it now spread and changed to accommodate different regions. Rough sawn wood construction, log picnic tables, stone walls and hand carved signs provide the imagery for the rural park in every corner of the United States today. The years have taken their toll on the work of the CCC, however. In many cases the design quality has been diluted by unattractive additions and by mass production of park furnishings and lack of application of the traditional craft skills.

The Moses legacy is more of an urban phenomenon which was based on intensive development of facilities for active recreation. This is worth emulating for urban centers where a system wide approach designed to handle large numbers of people is a requirement. Rustic facilities are less appropriate in urban settings and cannot stand up to heavy use. Many urban parks originally built in the rustic style could benefit by redesign in line with the sophisticated design qualities of Robert Moses' projects.

NOTES

1. *Park and Recreation Structures,* Introduction, U. S. Dept. of the Interior, National Park Service, 1938; reprt. 1944, U. S. Govt. Printing Office.

2. Robert A. Caro, *The Power Broker: Robert Moses and the Fall of New York* (New York: Alfred A. Knopf, 1974), p. 337.

3. "Barriers, Walls, and Fences," *Park and Recreation Structures* 91944), p. 2.

4. "Comfort Stations and Privies," Ibid., p. 19.

5. "Bridges," Ibid., p. 7.

6. "Drinking Fountains and Water Supply," Ibid., p. 22.

7. *Nomination Form: National Register of Historic Places, U. S. Dept. of the Interior,* James B. Jones & Claudette Stager, Historic Preservation Specialists, Tennessee Historical Commission, Nashville, Tennessee, 1986, Section E, p. 6.

8. Caro, p. 145.

The Best Laid Plans:
Robert Moses and the Making of Metroland
Mollie Keller

Two factors, it seemed to Robert Moses, newly appointed chief of the Long Island State Park Commission in 1924, made Long Island the natural and inevitable playground for metropolitan New York. Its 475 miles of beaches began less than thirty miles from Columbus Circle, and its lack of any arterial traffic routes promised to keep it free from any large-scale commercial development. Fired by his progressive faith in the ability of parks to keep the city's huddled middle and working classes breathing free, and inspired by the golf courses and summer hotels he found on the Island when he first moved to Babylon in 1922, Moses began accumulating seashore and meadowland, clear lakes and piney forests for the constellation of parks and parkways that by 1940 would be the jewel in the crown of the state park system, and the marvel of the western world.[1]

But Long Island never did become the enormous "recreational community" Moses planned. His beaches, glades, and playing fields became instead a precious oasis in the jumbled residential, commercial, and industrial sprawl we cope with today. Had Moses really looked at his promised land, he might have understood that he had about as great a chance of shaping Long Island to his will as King Canute did at stopping the tides. For by the time Moses put on his hard hat, Long Island had already reinvented itself as the Sunrise Homeland.

In 1877, a newly expanded and consolidated Long Island Railroad looked about for more customers, and hit upon the idea of selling the island as a vacationland. In a yearly series of illustrated, hyperbolic pamphlets, the railroad called "the attention of the overcrowded metropolis to the fact that within a few minutes' travel from its border . . . lies a vast area of country, upon which nature seems to have showered her choicest favors." These lists of points of interest along the line also offered visitors such useful information as the fares, the length of the trip, the number of trains, the "GOOD HOTELS and BOARDING HOUSES within a distance of five miles of the Depots; the DENOMINATION OF EACH CHURCH, and attractions of the Various Places," as well as descriptions of "the BATHING, BOATING, FISHING, SHOOTING, COST OF LIVING, & C." By the early eighties an extensive hotel network covered the island, ready to receive and restore hot, tired, stressed New Yorkers desperate to escape from "brick and mortardom."[2]

Relief from the city summer could be found both near and far. The beautiful people of the early nineteenth century had made Far Rockaway the "in" spot for bathing, and many of the "careworn brokers" of the century's end still flocked there to "inhale the purest of Oxygen and banish from [their] thoughts for the time being the fluctuation of stock." They also went a little farther east to sojourn in the grand hotels and modest boarding houses facing the white sands and grey-green waters at Manhattan Beach, where the Long Beach Estates Company had spent millions of dollars building hotels, casinos, and several miles of boardwalk for a second Atlantic City.[3]

Vacationers could actually be happy anywhere on the Island. The hills and harbors of the North Shore welcomed guests on a more intimate scale. Sea Cliff, Stony Brook, and Shoreham all invited city families to stay in their guest homes and furnished cottages, sail among the coves and inlets, watch birds along the shore, and picnic in the meadows. Bungalow colonies guarded the South Shore from Freeport to Patchogue and beyond, offering a more private alternative to hotel life. The extreme eastern end of the island had already settled into its twentieth century role. Westhampton, reported the railroad in 1877, was gaining as a resort, and "Quogue has been celebrated as a watering place for over half a century." Even the middle of the island, long looked upon as the local version of the Great American Desert, lured tourists. Hicksville, a railroad junction just south of the fabled Wheatley Hills, boasted three hotels in 1896. One of them, the American, billed itself as "The Sportsmen's Hotel," and provided its guests with "thoroughbred pointers, Irish setters and hounds," as well as "hacking at reasonable prices."[4]

Several early resorts, seeking their own niche in a crowded market, adopted the motto *mens sana in corpore sano*. They had more than fresh air for their clientele. For example, Point O'Woods on the sandbar now known as Fire Island began its life as a Chautauqua colony dedicated to high thinking and sober living. Several other Long Island towns owed their vitality to religion. Merrick had large camp meeting grounds, as did Jamesport, and Shelter Island hosted several revivals each season before it restyled itself as "The American Naples" in the 1920s.[5]

By the turn of the century more and more *patresfamilias*, searching for a "Salubrious Summer home . . . in proximity to New York, [with] . . . a low temperature, healthful recreation, and freedom from malaria," had bought the picture the promoters painted, and discovered that Long Island was more than "a sandy waste dotted with scrub oak and mosquitoes." It was more than gingerbread hotels, salt-water fishing, and forty golf courses, too. Long Island had two great advantages over any other vacation spot: proximity and accessibility. Unlike at the New Jersey Shore, or Newport, or the Maine woods, the whole family could enjoy a summer on Long Island—thanks to the railroad. Rail service had become dependable enough by the Civil War to make weekend commuting possible. Twenty years later it was good enough to carry Island "ladies" in for a day of "shopping or enjoy[ing] amusements in the great city," and other residents for an evening of visiting theatres and friends, or attending concerts or lectures. By 1900, when the Long Island Railroad became part of the Pennsylvania system, its frequent, forty mile an hour trains were reliable enough to make it "feasible and agreeable for a businessman to be at his counting house in town during the day, and to reach his Summer home before nightfall." Parlor cars, complete with porters and smoking compartments, and private cars attached for the convenience of commuters from a particular station, also eased the journey between one's city desk and country seat.[6]

Within the next ten years the opening of the East River tunnels and the grand Pennsylvania Station, as well as the electrification of the line beyond the city limits, had made a home on Long Island even more "feasible and agreeable," not only to millionaires and the well-to-do, but also to "the prudent wage earner who must needs get the most comfort for the least money." And not just for the summer, either. Long Island's season, which had always lasted longer than, say, Long Branch's, now began to stretch beyond November into the following spring—encouraged, of course, by a railroad anxious to secure year-round ridership to finance its improvements.[7]

Railroad publicity now touted a new vision of Long Island— that of a wonderful place to live. "Public spirited citizens who have no property interest to be subserved by such declarations, and students of sociology who decry the overcrowded state of Manhattan [as] a condition that retards the development of citizenship, have been pointing for many years to the wide expanses of Long Island as a place for residences," solemnly pronounced one copywriter. Playing on New Yorkers' fears and prejudices, the railroad contrasted the ever-exploding size of the anonymous city and its "crowded tenements" with Long Island's "succession of neat communities" and "little towns," each one proud of its own churches, schools, libraries, and golf courses, as well as its inhabitants' English ancestry. A typical *New York Times* ad—this one titled "Country Life"—promised that Long Island could provide it all for "those who wish to have a home outside of the crowded city." The sell became harder after the opening of Penn Station. "No matter how long a man lives in a hotel it cannot be a home," the railroad warned before assuring members of the new business class that every man "of moderate means and quiet tastes" could have his own home and garden in which to protect his family from "the noisy, bustling and immoral city"—and still be only forty miles from his office. Still another ad gloomily observed that "the city man does not know what 'living' is. There is a sameness about living in a city that soon wears on one and brings about discontent." (One wonders what Dr. Johnson would have made of that!) The solution to the malaise? Move to Long Island! The railroad stated its case most bluntly and prophetically in its 1915 publication, *Long Island and Real Life*. "Long Island goes in first for the comforts of life, and the gingerbread can come afterwards. It is well known, and will become still better known, for its colonies, where building *en masse* and modern business methods have carried the art of living, for persons of moderate means, to very nearly its highest possibilities."[8]

Real estate brokers and developers were quick to echo and amplify the railroad's song. News articles in the *New York Times*— sometimes even a whole section of the Sunday paper—

rhapsodized about the new dawn in the sunrise homeland. These stories evoked almost irresistible images of "breeze-swept beaches" and "wooded hills," of country clubs and yacht clubs and hunt clubs, and at the same time reassured skeptical readers of the efficacy of the third-rail service, the availability of homes for "the home-builder of lesser means," and the rapid extermination of "that persistent pest," the Long Island mosquito. Developers published their reasons why the island was a good investment, and their optimistic predictions about property values. Suburban residences in places like Great Neck, Babylon, and Huntington were photographed and described with the care usually reserved for brides. And the planning, construction, or opening of a new home center or subdivision was always worth a column or two.[9]

"Let's build a little bungalow in Quogue; In Yaphank or in Hicksville or Patchogue" urged a popular song of 1917. By then it was fairly easy to do. Buyers could go to Bay Shore, where the T. B. Ackerson Company was improving its seven hundred acres Brightwaters development with Venetian bridges, a Stone Cascade, Roman Stone Pagodas, and "numbers of cosey [sic] ... Cottages, Chalets, and Semi-Bungalows, for all-year-round homes" from $2,500 and up. Or to Manhasset to see the $5–20,000 houses being built by the Plandome Land Company. If they were very picky they could consult Fitch H. Medbury about those "country seats" at "The Lands Called Shoreham," which, he promised in capital letters, are "FAR ENOUGH AWAY from the City of New York so there is NO DANGER of the UNDESIRABLE CLASSES ever enroaching upon the residents. . . ." They could also check the Long Island Realty Company's "Small Farms for Suburbanites," the Brentwood Realty Company's "very attractive Bungalows," or, at the top of the scale, Belle Terre Estates' neighborhood of mansions which was giving new cachet to the old town of Port Jefferson.[10]

The promotions and advertising worked. Long Island boomed. Many came, saw, and were conquered by the suburban alternative to rent receipts. Nassau County's population grew steadily between 1890 and 1920, tripling from 41,009 to 126,120; Suffolk's grew from 62,491 to 110,246. Between 1920 and 1925 Nassau continued to expand nine times faster than it had in the previous five years. The Long Island Lighting Company serviced

100,00 more gas customers in 1925 than in 1910, and 93,000 more electricity users. Seventy-one thousand dwellings went up on Long Island between 1912 and 1922. And traffic on the Long Island Railroad increased, too, from 4,676 commuters a month in 1905, to 50,000 in 1922. The island really was becoming the "homeland of the metropolis."[11]

It was toward this brainchild of the railroad, this summer resort become suburbia, that Robert Moses turned his dreamer's eye when he contemplated the steamy, crowded streets of Manhattan in 1920. He did not pay much attention to the lot selling and home building going on there, however. Because of its nearness to the city, its shore line, and its lack of through routes, Long Island was obviously, he decided, destined to be a "place for people to live and play, mostly play," an escape hatch for the city. But watching the island's narrow roads being choked each summer Sunday by more than one hundred thousand cars, each lured eastward on what was viewed as a "destructive exodus" from the city by advertising, reputation, and a longing for cool breezes, he did not see the railroad's "Long Island; The Land of Pastimes," or "Long Island: The Land of Opportunity." He saw "Long Island: The Land of Greed." He saw acres of open land being bought and sold by the square foot; private fences enclosing enough space to house a village; "no trespassing" signs warning bathers from the beaches. And he determined that it did not have to be that way. Long Island's blessings could be enjoyed, both by its residents and by the ever-growing "vast throngs of pleasure seekers" they feared, simply by putting more of those blessings under public control and then building roads to them.[12]

The saga of how he actually built those roads and playgrounds is too familiar for retelling here. What is more important is their effect on Long Island's development.

Moses' roads did not turn the Island into a 120 mile long resort. Far too many people had decided that Long Island was destined to be a place for people to live and play, mostly live. Consequently, Moses' roads had the same effect as the extension and electrification of the railroad. "Parkway Will Boom L. I. South Shore," heralded the *Times* in September, 1926; two months later it announced massive development plans for Montauk. Real estate brokers noted with joy the availability of desirable homesites farther and farther from the railroad, and closer and closer to the parkways. The cross island routes joining the Northern and Southern State Parkways, and the proposed Triborough Bridge linking Long Island to the rest of the state, further fed the suburban frenzy by opening new towns to speculation and development, first at the entrance ramps, and then into the potato fields between them. The locals who had been so vocal about the plague of locusts Moses was calling upon them now complained that the parkways' limited entrances and exits made it hard for city people to patronize the Island's shops and restaurants en route to the beach. And others quietly wrote the Commissioner about land they thought he might be able to use, seeing in his plans both personal gain and a boost to the otherwise "long and wearisome operation" of developing new parts of the island.[13]

By 1930 Long Island was reaping what Moses had sown. Nassau County's population had almost trebled again to 303,053, while Suffolk's had reached a more modest 161,055. Moses, proud of his parks, was neither surprised nor alarmed by this growth. It is "a ridiculous proposition," he wrote, to suppose "that traffic can be kept back" and "subdivisions prevented." But he remained convinced that with "intelligent planning ... especially ... as to traffic arteries . . . the character of the country can be measurably retained."[14]

The character of the country was not measurably retained, however. Why? Because Moses' intelligent planning had no new idea behind it; it fact, it had an old one. Moses bought the vision of Long Island the Vacationland that had been articulated at least as early as 1877, and devoted his energies to expanding and decommercializing that dream. While he acknowledged the newer, competing commercial vision of Long Island the Homeland, he underestimated its strength and influence, and so did not wage war against those who were fencing in house lots as he did against those who fenced in beaches. His beautiful string of parks was really his testament to a Long Island past. He did not understand the appeal of the Long Island present, or that no one, not even Robert Moses, could build an old world upon a new.

NOTES

1. Robert A. Caro, *The Power Broker* (New York; Alfred A. Knopf, 1974), p. 275; "Robert (Or-I'll Resign) Moses," *Fortune*, June, 1938; "Pattern for Parks," *Architectural Forum*, December, 1936, p. 493.

2. Long Island Railroad, *Long Island And Where To Go!* (New York, 1877), p. 3; Marilyn E. Weigold, *The American Mediterranean: An Environmental, Economic and Social History of Long Island Sound* (Port Washington, NY: Kennikat Press, 1974), pp. 57-58.

3. Ralph Henry Gabriel, *The Evolution of Long Island* (New Haven: Yale University Press, 1921), p. 172; *Where To Go!*, p. 165; Long Island Railroad, *Long Island Illustrated 1882*, passim; *New York Times*, May 31, 1908.

4. *Where To Go!*, p. 85; Richard and Anne Evers, "Today and Yesterday," unpublished ms. at the Gregory Museum, Hicksville, NY.

5. *Where To Go!*, pp. 69, 81, 181; Long Island Railroad and Long Island Real Estate Board, *Long Island: The Sunrise Homeland* (New York, 1927), passim.

6. *Long Island Illustrated 1882*, Introductory, p. 1; Long Island Railroad, *The Beauties of Long Island* (New York, 1895), p. 5; Weigold, p. 60; *Long Island Summer Resorts Guide and Directory 1878*, p. 2; *Where To Go!*, pp. 114, 133; Long Island Railroad, *Long Island Illustrated 1907*, p. 121.

7. *New York Times*, April 25, 1909, April 10, May 14, 1922; Long Island Railroad, *Long Island Illustrated 1900*, p. 12.

8. *New York Times*, January 10, 1909, April 25, 1909, September 4, 1910, April 28, 1912, April 13, 1913; Long Island Railroad, *Long Island and Real Life* (New York, 1915), p. 7.

9. See, for example, the *New York Times* for May 31, 1908, February 18, 1912, and passim.

10. Jerome Kern and P. G. Wodehouse, "Bungalow in Quogue," 1917; *New York Times*, April 25, 1909, May 29, 1910, April 28, 1912; Long Island Railroad, *Long Island Resorts 1912, Long Island and Real Life 1915, 1916*, passim.

11. *Brooklyn Daily Eagle Almanac*, 1918, p. 82; Population Folder, Population Pictorial and Clippings Envelopes, and Box 8, Long Island Banks 1929-30, Long Island Studies Institute, Hofstra University; Long Island Lighting Company, *The Story of Our Twenty-Five Years of Service to Long Island, 1911-1936* (1936), p. 37; *New York Times*, January 28, 1917, November 4, 1920. See also French Strother, "Long Island—New York's Largest Child," *The World's Work LV* (April, 1928), pp. 628-639, for a description of Long Island in the early 1920s.

12. *New York Times*, November 26, 1922; Weigold, pp. 111, 107; *Power Broker*, p. 275; Trubee Davison in *East Norwich Enterprise*, January

26, 1924, Box 3, Folder Personal 1919–26, Long Island, and Robert Moses to Franklin D. Roosevelt, January 23, 1928, Box 1, Folder Correspondence 1924–33, Robert Moses Papers, Manuscripts and Archives Division, New York Public Library.

13. *New York Times,* September 5, 1926, November 7, 1926, May 10, 1925, August 21, 1910, October 10, 1926, and every Sunday real estate section during those years; *New York Herald Tribune,* December 28, 1925, June 15, 1925; Moses Greenwood to Robert Moses, February 18, 1924, James A. S. Gregg to Alfred E. Smith, March 6, 1924, James A. S. Gregg to Robert Moses, April 1, 1924, Box 3, Folder Long Island State Park Commission 1924, Robert Moses Papers, Manuscripts and Archives Division, New York Public Library.

14. Long Island Real Estate Board, *Long Island: The Sunrise Homeland 1931,* pp. 63, 113; Robert Moses to Franklin D. Roosevelt, March 12, 1928, Box 4, Folder FDR (1928), Robert Moses Papers, Manuscripts and Archives Division, New York Public Library.

Courtesy of Triborough Bridge and Tunnel Authority
Bronx-Whitestone Bridge with addition of strengthening trusses above roadway

The Public Works of Aymar Embury II in New York City and Long Island

Peter S. Kaufman

The public works of Aymar Embury II in New York City and Long Island span a panorama from the Verrazano Narrows bridge eastward to the farthest extent of Long Island at East Hampton, a distance of 125 miles. They include dozens of bridges within and among all five boroughs of the city, huge pool complexes throughout the city, two public spaces in the heart of Manhattan (Bryant Park and Herald Square Plaza), both the Central Park and Prospect Park zoos, the permanent New York City building at the 1939 New York World's Fair, and what Embury himself called his "most interesting commission," the campus of Hofstra University in Hempstead, Long Island. This is quite a legacy for a man who never attended architecture school; moreover, it represents only a slice of Embury's total output as an architect, comprising hundreds of buildings throughout the eastern United States.

An engineer by training, Embury was born in New York City on June 15, 1880, the son of Aymar Embury, an attorney, and Fannie Miller (Bates) Embury. A precocious child, he was ready for college at the age of fourteen, by his own account, but delayed entrance into Princeton until just past his sixteenth birthday. Embury acquired his architectural training in New York City through apprenticeship. At a time when he considered himself merely "a draftsman with a job," his big break came, in 1905, when he won not just first prize but second prize as well in a contest held by the Garden City Company for a modest country house to be built in Garden City, Long Island. This led to numerous country house commissions in the New York metropolitan region.

By the time of World War I, Embury was well-established as an architect and, through his formidable publishing record, as an historian, two roles which were closely intertwined in his mind. After the war Embury became caught up in the nation-wide building boom of the 1920s, attracting a wide range of commissions as far away as North Carolina, Alabama, and Michigan, including many college buildings.

When the Great Depression hit, putting many architects out of business, Embury opened a new chapter in his career as chief and consulting architect to the leading public works agencies of New York City: the Port Authority of New York, the Triborough Bridge and Tunnel Authority, and the New York City Parks Department. These agencies were beehives of activity during the New Deal Era, engaged in the design and construction of hundreds of parks, bridges, roadways, and recreational facilities throughout the city, mostly under the direction of Robert Moses. By his own account, Embury supervised the design of over 600 of these structures including 200 "up to the sketch stage."

Verrazano-Narrows Bridge from Brooklyn

Courtesy Triborough Bridge and Tunnel Authority

By far the most conspicuous of these structures were the bridges he executed for the Triborough Bridge and Tunnel Authority. Among these, the most celebrated was the Bronx-Whitestone (1937–1939), a sliver of steel shot across Long Island Sound like a flare in record time for the opening of the New York World's Fair in 1939. It represents the apogee of attenuated bridge design for the period, embodying a girder depth-to-span ration of 1 to 210, later thickened by the addition of strengthening trusses which mar the original thinness of the bridge. The roadbed bears plate girders instead of trusses,and there is no wind bracing between the legs of the towers near the roadway. The towers, with their unusually high arches and flattened piers, accentuate the elegance of the design. The designers conceived of the towers as single enormous units reinforced at the sides by steel buttresses. They are battered, that is, slightly slanted, only in the longitudinal direction of the bridge, and their only decoration is the gallery at the top and the vertical stiffeners which actually serve a structural function.

As the longest suspension bridge in the world when it was built, the Verrazano Narrows bridge carried the design of the Bronx-Whitestone to a dramatic conclusion at the mouth of New York harbor. Resolutely classical in its use of the semi-circular arch in the towers, it signals a climax of classicism for New York City, and is often compared to the Golden Gate bridge in San Francisco which it matches in symbolic importance and exceeds in span by only sixty feet.

In contrast to these classicistic works, the Triborough Bridge is a complicated engineering marvel connecting Manhattan, Queens, the Bronx, and several islands in the middle of the East River. The first vehicular crossing of the East River north of Fifty-ninth Street, it extends a full 17 miles in length including all the approach roadways.

Embury's other major contribution to the public architecture of New York City in the New Deal Era are the five huge pool complexes built, one in each of the city's boroughs, beginning in 1935. For these buildings he chose a round-arched Romanesque style, recalling the Romanesque Revival of Henry Hobson Richardson as well as America's great tradition of public armory and arsenal architecture.

The permanent New York City building at the 1939 World's

Fair forms a fitting conclusion to Embury's New York City public works, for it is his largest and most conspicuous public building, standing next to the Grand Central Parkway in Queens and stretching almost a football field in length. The present building bears the marks of renovation carried out by the architect Daniel Chait in preparation for the 1964 World's Fair. These obscure the original Greek austerity of the building, and it is hoped that the present renovation by architect Raphael Vinoly may restore some of this original feeling in tune with the Post-Modern present.

Embury's most important commission on Long Island was the design of the Hofstra University campus in Hempstead, which began in 1936 as the Long Island extension of New York University. The way he was chosen for this design says a great deal about American architectural politics in the 1930s. New York University's architectural advisor was Fiske Kimball, a distinguished architect and historian of architecture, and his first recommendation for the commission was William Lescaze, a French emigre

Triborough Bridge complex from Queens showing
Hell Gate Railroad Bridge and trestle on right

Courtesy of Triborough Bridge and Tunnel Authority

architect living in New York who practiced in the European modernist mode. The college's board of advisors found his designs too modern, and Embury was ushered in immediately as a more traditional designer who was experienced in academic buildings and knowledgeable about Long Island architecture in particular.

Embury remained with the college until 1963, guiding its architectural development in a consistent and disciplined Neoclassical manner for almost three full decades. He thereby created one of the most distinguished academic environments of the period, a veritable museum of Beaux Arts architecture dating from the middle third of the twentieth century. As in the University of Virginia campus in Charlottesville designed by Thomas Jefferson, each building is unique, yet the ensemble is united by a common institutional scale (never exceeding three stories) and common building materials consisting of pink and buff-colored brick with limestone trim. Complemented by arboretum-like grounds and organized into pedestrian-scaled quadrangles, this campus breathes the air of the eighteenth century. It is calm, cool, and classificatory—refined, restrained, and above all rational.

Courtesy Hofstra University Archives

Hofstra University campus, c. 1955

In conclusion, Aymar Embury II was a member of an Edwardian generation of architects which inherited the mantle of historical revivalism from the nineteenth century, yet faced the increasing industrialization of architectural form in the twentieth century. He was well prepared to effect a marriage between the two as an architectural epicure by heart and an engineer by training. Like most progressive architects of his day, he chose a middle-of-the-road approach, steadily refining and streamlining historical forms over the course of his career until they looked almost modern. Still, except in his engineering works, he never abandoned the most basic premises of traditional, academic architecture: the relevance of historical forms, the primacy of unified planning, and the appearance of bearing wall construction. Embury bridged more that just shorelines in his career; he bridged the eighteenth century and the twentieth, engineering and architecture, taste and traffic.

BIBLIOGRAPHY

Saylor, Henry H., ed. *Country Houses by Aymar Embury II.* Garden City, N.Y.: Doubleday, Page, 1914.

Not a House but a Home: Designs by Aymar Embury II. Little Rock, Arkansas: Arkansas Soft Pine Bureau, 1916.

Books by Aymar Embury:

One Hundred Country Houses: Modern American Examples N.Y.: Century Co., 1909.

The Dutch Colonial House. N.Y.: McBride, Nast, 1913.

Early American Churches. Garden City, N.Y.: Doubleday, Page, 1914.

Architecture in American Country Homes. N.Y.: Mentor Assoc., 1915.

The Livable House, Its Plan & Design. N.Y.: Moffat, Yard, 1917.

English Architecture As Source Material. N.Y.: Ludowici-Celadon, 1929.

Architecture of Denmark & Her Former Provinces. N.Y.: Ludowici-Celadon, 1939.

Quotations within the text are to autobiographical reminiscences among Embury's professional papers housed in the Syracuse University Library.

Contributors

Editor

JOANN P. KRIEG, who directed the 1988 Moses Conference, is an Associate Professor of English and American Studies, Hofstra University. She has authored and edited a number of works, including two publications from the Institute's 1986 conference on Long Island Studies: *To Know the Place: Teaching Local History* (1986) and *Evoking a Sense of Place* (1988).

Contributors

PETER BALES is a history teacher at the Portledge School in Locust Valley, N.Y., and a doctoral candidate in history at SUNY/Stony Brook. His dissertation topic is Nelson Rockefeller's governmental and business dealings with Latin America.

JOHN A. BLACK is a Professor of Biology at Suffolk Community College, Selden, N.Y. He is the author of *Water Pollution Technology* (1977) and *Oceans and Coasts: An Introduction to Oceanography* (1986), as well as numerous papers on coastal dynamics.

FRANK B. BURGGRAF is a Professor of Landscape Architecture at the University of Arkansas in Fayetteville. He is a fellow of the American Society of Landscape Architects, and for ten years was employed by the State of New York Public Service Committee in the area of environmental planning.

JAMESON W. DOIG is Professor of Politics and Public Affairs, Princeton University, and Director of Graduate Studies in the Department of Politics. He is author of *Metropolitan Transportation Politics and the New York Region* (1966), co-author of *New York: The Politics of Urban Regional Development* (1982) and of *Leadership and Innovation: A Biographical Perspective on Entrepreneurs in Government* (1987).

HELEN A. HARRISON is art historian, curator, and journalist specializing in twentieth-century American art. She organized The Queens Museum 1980 exhibit, "Dawn of a New Day: The New York World's Fair, 1939/40." Currently she is an art critic for the Long Island Weekly section of *The New York Times* and Curator of Guild Hall Museum in East Hampton.

KENNETH T. JACKSON is Mellon Professor of History and Social Sciences at Columbia University. He won the Bancroft and Parkman prizes for *Crabgrass Frontier: The Suburbanization of the United States* (1986), and has just completed *Silent Cities: The Evolution of the American Cemetery* (1989).

PETER S. KAUFMAN, formerly a member of faculties in New York institutions, now teaches architectural history at the Florida A&M University School of Architecture in Tallahassee. He has lectured and published widely on modern American architectural history, and curated the exhibit "Designing the Moses Era: The Public Works of Aymar Embury" which was part of Hofstra University's 1988 conference on Robert Moses.

MOLLIE KELLER is an independent historian who has been researcher, writer, archivist, planner, and curator for clients ranging from the United States Army to local historical societies. The author of several biographies for young adult readers, she is currently completing a doctoral dissertation at New York University on "Levittown and the Transformation of the Metropolis."

PETER L. KRAMER is Chairman of the Advisory Committee on the Long Island State Parks and the Friends of Jones Beach, Inc. He is a partner in the Long Island and New York City law firm of Lysaght, Lysaght & Kramer. He is also a long-time seasonal supervisor at Jones Beach State Park.

JEFFREY A. KROESSLER is the author of *A Guide to Historical Map Resources For Greater New York,* as well as several articles on the history of Queens County. He has curated important exhibits for the Queens Historical Society, most recently, "Relief, Recovery, and Reform: The Great Depression and New Deal in Queens." He is, at present, a doctoral candidate in history at the City University of New York Graduate Center.

J. LANCE MALLAMO is Director of Historic Services and County Historian for Suffolk County, N.Y. He supervises the preservation of all landmark structures owned by Suffolk County and serves on the Board of Directors of numerous historical organizations on Long Island. Mr. Mallamo has been at the forefront of efforts to preserve early Long Island roadways and roadside development.

KAREN E. MARKOE teaches in the Department of History at the State University of New York Maritime College. In 1986 she was a participant in a National Endowment for the Humanities seminar on New York City history.

ROBERT A. MILLER is an audio-visual technician at the Queens Borough Public Library, Jamaica, N.Y. He is a frequent lecturer on Long Island's maritime heritage and roadways.

NATALIE A. NAYLOR is a Professor at Hofstra University, Teaching Fellow in New College, and Director of the Long Island Studies Institute. She teaches courses in various aspects of American social history and has published a number of articles in educational and local history.

DAVID OATS is Editor of the *Tribune,* a Queens County, N.Y. weekly newspaper. He is former Chair of the Queens County Chamber of Commerce and now heads a citizens advisory committee on Flushing Meadows-Corona Park, Queens County.

DAVID C. PERRY is Albert A. Levin Professor of Urban Studies and Public Service at Cleveland State University, and Professor of Planning and Design at State University of New York, Buffalo. He has co-authored *The Rise of the Sunbelt Cities* and several articles on

Robert Moses. Presently he is engaged in a research project based on Moses' public and private papers.

KAREN L. ROLLET is an Assistant Professor of Landscape Architecture at the University of Arkansas, Fayetteville. She is presently working with Frank B. Burggraf on a study, "Design Harmony of Man-Made Elements in Natural Settings," under a grant from the Arkansas Historical Preservation Program.

GEORGE STEVENS is Assistant Professor of History at Dutchess Community College, Poughkeepsie, N.Y. He has also taught at Cornell University's School of Industrial and Labor Relations.

The Long Island Studies Institute

The Long Island Studies Institute at Hofstra University was established in 1985, when the Nassau County Museum Reference Library moved to Hofstra, combining with Hofstra's New York State History collection to create a major resource for the study of Long Island local and regional history. The Institute, on the ninth floor of the Axinn Library, also houses the historical research offices of the Nassau County Historian and Division of Museum Services.

The Long Island Studies Institute has sponsored programs, symposia, conferences, and publications to enhance awareness of Long Island's rich heritage. The 1986 conference on Long Island Studies resulted in two publications: *To Know the Place: Teaching Local History* (1987) and *Evoking a Sense of Place* (1988). "Suburbia Re-Examined," the Institute's 1987 conference commemorating the 40th anniversary of Levittown, has publications forthcoming in 1989. For information on conferences and publications, contact the Long Island Studies Institute, Hofstra University, Hempstead, NY 11550; (516) 560–5092.

Index

Numbers in *italics* refer to illustrations

Adams, John Cranford, 176, 177, 178, 179, 180, 181, 182–83, 184
Adams, Thomas, 136–137
"American Real Estate Industry and National Housing Policy" (Marc A. Weiss), 16
Ammann, O. H., 104
Astoria Park and Pool. *See* Moses, Robert, N.Y.C. parks
Battle, George, 75
"Bayville-Rye Bridge." *See* Moses, Robert, bridges
Belt Parkway. *See* Moses, Robert, parkways
Bethpage State Park. *See* Moses, Robert, N.Y. State parks
Bill, Hawthorn, 138
Blakelock, Chester R., 178–79, 180
Blumenfeld, Myron H., 15
Bronx-Whitestone Bridge. *See* Moses, Robert, bridges
Brooklyn-Battery Tunnel, 21, 36
Brooklyn-Queens Expressway. *See* Moses, Robert, parkways
Bruckner Expressway. *See* Moses, Robert, parkways
Bryant, William Cullen, 29
Burnham, Daniel, 16
Canarsie Beach Park. *See* Moses, Robert, N.Y.C. parks
Caro, Robert A.
    L.I. Studies Institute conference speaker, 13–14
    refuted, 14, 16–17, 23–29, 32, 41–43, 47, 57, 65
    refuted by Moses. *See* Moses, Robert, on Caro
Chait, Daniel, 216
Civilian Conservation Corps (CCC) Parks, 191–94, *193*, 195, 196–99, *197*, *199*, 200
Clarke, Gilmore, 96–97
Clearview Expressway. *See* Moses, Robert, parkways
Corona Dumps, 91–92, *92*, 93, 94, *94*, 103, 105, 110–12
Crabgrass Frontier (Jackson), 14, 27
Cross Bay Bridge. *See* Moses, Robert, bridges
Cross Bronx Expressway. *See* Moses, Robert, parkways
Dewey, Thomas E., 21, 61
Doughty, Wilbur, 136
Edel, Leon, 31, 32
Embury, Aymar, II, 15, 179–80, 181–82, 213–17
FDR Drive. *See* Moses, Robert, parkways
Federal Housing Administration, 28, 42, 44
"Fire Island Jetty" (Cyril Galvin), 16
Fire Island State Park. *See* Moses, Robert, N.Y. State parks
Flushing Meadow Park. *See* Moses, Robert, N.Y.C. parks
Gidlund, Leonara, paper describing Moses' public papers, 1934–60, 16
Gowanus Expressway. *See* Moses, Robert, parkways

Grand Central Parkway. *See* Moses, Robert, parkways
Great Gatsby, The (Fitzgerald), 91, 106, 110
Green, Andrew Haswell, 29
Guggenheim, Harry, 62
Harlem River Drive. *See* Moses, Robert, parkways
Harriman, Averell, W., 21
Heckscher, August, 48
Heckscher State Park. *See* Moses, Robert, N.Y. State parks
Hempstead Lake State Park. *See* Moses, Robert, N.Y. State parks
Henry Hudson Bridge. *See* Moses, Robert, bridges
Henry Hudson Parkway. *See* Moses, Robert, parkways
Hither Hills State Park. *See* Moses, Robert, N.Y. State parks
Hoey, James, 71, 74
Hofstra University
   architecture, 213, 216–17
   campus, *217*
   Board of Trustees, 1943–56, 175–88
Hutchinson River Parkway. *See* Moses, Robert, parkways
"Impact of the Robert Moses Power Plant on Industrial Location, The" (Iris Berman), 16
Interborough Parkway. *See* Moses, Robert, parkways
Jackson, Kenneth T., 14, 16, 43, 44, 51–52
Jacobs, Jane, 23, 52
Jamaica Bay Wildlife Refuge. *See* Moses, Robert, public works
Jones Beach State Park. *See* Moses, Robert, N.Y. State parks
Jones Beach Theatre. *See* Moses, Robert, N.Y. State parks
"Joseph Jenson, the Robert Moses of California" (Fred W. Viehe), 16
Kaufman, Peter, 15
Kennedy, John F., 110

Kern, Paul, 38
Kramer, Peter L., 16
LaGuardia, Fiorello, 21, 24, 38, 50, 60, 75, 101, 102, 112, 143
Lehman, Herbert, H., 21
Lehman, Orin, 15
Lincoln Center for the Performing Arts. *See* Moses, Robert, public works
Lindsay, John V., 21, 48, 114
Lippman, Walter, 36
Loeser, Paul, 76
Long Island Expressway. *See* Moses, Robert, parkways
Long Island Motor Parkway, 152–54, *153, 155, 157,* 155, 156–58, 160
Long Island Railroad, 203, 205, 206–07
Long Island State Park Headquarters, *123*
Long Island Studies Institute, 13, 16
Major Deegan Expressway. *See* Moses, Robert, parkways
Marine Parkway. *See* Moses, Robert, parkways
McAneny, George, 93, 96
McCarthy, Michael P., 16
McGoldrick, Joseph, 60
Meadowbrook Parkway. *See* Moses, Robert, parkways
Metropolitan Transportation Authority (MTA), 83, 84, 86, 114
Montauk State Park. *See* Moses, Robert, N.Y. State parks
Moses' Long Island, *90*
"Moses men," 22
Moses, Robert:
   Bethpage Park Authority, chairman, 9
   bridges
      "Bayville-Rye," 79–87
      Bronx-Whitestone, 21, 75, 76, 79, 102, 107, 113, *212,* 215
      Cross Bay, 21
      Henry Hudson, 21
      Robert Moses, *126*

Moses, Robert: bridges (continued)
  Throgs Neck, 21, 29, 58, 79
  Triborough, 22, 36, 71, 74, 75, 79, 102, 103, 111, 209, 215, *216*
  Verrazano Narrows, 21, 58, 65, *128*, 213, *214*, 215
City Airport Authority, commissioner, 60–64
education, 9, 39–40
environmentalist, 92, 105, 106, 138, 139, 141–48, 161
gubernatorial candidate, 9
Henry Hudson Parkway Authority, 9
Hofstra College, trustee, 9, 175–85
Jones Beach State Parkway Authority, chairman, 9
Lincoln Center for the Performing Arts, director, 10
Long Island State Parks Commission, president, 9, 75, 76, 137–38, 142, 144–45, 146, 166, 203
Marine Parkway Authority, 9
and the media, 38–39, 40
Newsday columnist, 81, 82, 137
N.Y.C. Parks
  Astoria Park and Pool, 102, 103, 106
  Canarsie Beach, 106
  Flushing Meadow, 91, *95*, 95–96, *98*, 98, 109, 114, 115
  Orchard Beach, 21
N.Y.C. Parks, commissioner, 9, 21, 101–2, 113
N.Y.C. Planning Commission, member, 9, 58
N.Y. Power Authority, chairman, 9
N.Y. Secretary of State, 9
N.Y. State Parks, 142–43, 144
  Bethpage, 16, *121*, *122*, 160, 170
  Fire Island, 135, 138–39, 142, 144

Moses, Robert:
  N.Y. State Parks (continued)
    Heckscher, *118*, *129*, 144
    Hempstead Lake, 144, 170
    Hither Hills, *126*, 143, 144
    Jones Beach, 21, 26, 29, *119*, *125*, 135–38, 144, 160, *168*, 169–74, *171*, *173*, *190*, 194–95, *195*, 196
    Jones Beach Theatre, *134*, 170
    Montauk, *132*, 144
    Orient Point, 143, 144
    Robert Moses, *120*
    Sunken Meadow, 144
    Valley Stream, *124*, 144
    Wildwood *124*
  on Robert A. Caro, 31, 49–50, 51
  parents of, 9
  parkways, 141–42, 144, 157, 160–61, 163, 208
    Belt, 23, 102, 107, 164
    Brooklyn-Queens Exp'wy, 23
    Bruckner Exp'wy, 23
    Clearview Exp'wy, 23
    Cross Bronx Exp'wy, 23, 27, 28, 39, 42
    FDR Drive, 23
    Gowanus Exp'wy, 23
    Grand Central, 23, 103, 113
    Harlem River Drive, 23
    Henry Hudson, 23
    history of, 151–58, 159, 160
    Hutchinson River, 23
    Interborough, 23, 103
    landscaping of, 164–65
    lighting of, 163–64
    Long Island Exp'wy, 23, 81, 153
    Major Deegan, 23, 103
    Marine, 22, 105, 106
    Meadowbrook, 23, 161
    Northern State, 23, 81, 144, 153, 157, 161, 164, 209
    Ocean, 142, 143, 164
    overpasses, 163
    Prospect Exp'wy, 23

Moses, Robert:
  parkways (continued)
    signage on, 164
    Southern State, 23, *127*, 144, 161, *162*, 163, 209
    Van Wyck Exp'wy, 23
    Wantagh State, 23, 144, 164
    West Side Highway, 23
    Whitestone, 23
  photographs of, *8, 20, 56*
  public housing, 21, 25, 37
    South Bronx, 25
  public works, 21, 22, 26, 69, 102, 103, 104, 143
    Jamaica Bay Wildlife Refuge, 143
    Lincoln Center for the Performing Arts, 22
    New York Coliseum, 69
    Riverside Park, 22, 27, 29
    Rockaway Improvement, 104–5, 106
    Shea Stadium, 22, *130*
    United Nations building, 69, 114
    World's Fair, 1939, 22, 93–98, 106–7, 112, 113, 114, *131*, 213, 215–16
    World's Fair, 1964, 22, 109–10, 114, *131*
  racism, 26–28, 29, 37, 38, 42
  State Council of Parks, chairman, 9
  Triborough Bridge Authority (TBA), chairman, 9, 70–71, 73, 74, 75, 76, 77, 102, 103, 104
  Triborough Bridge and Tunnel Authority (TBTA), chairman, 9, 38, 40–41, 73, 77, 79, 83–84, 113, 114, 214, 215
Moskowitz, Belle, 40
Mumford, Lewis, 22, 35, 52
New Deal, 72, 101–2, 103, 107, 214
Newsday. *See* Moses, Robert, *Newsday* columnist

New York Coliseum. *See* Moses, Robert, public works
N.Y. Port Authority, 29, 38, 57–65, 104, 105, 214
N.Y. World's Fair Corporation (1935), 93–94, 96, 97, 98
  Whalen, Grover, president, 94
Northern State Parkway. *See* Moses, Robert, parkways
Oats, David, 16
O'Brien, John, 71, 74
Ocean Parkway. *See* Moses, Robert, parkways
O'Dwyer, William, 60, 61, 62, 63, 64
Olmsted, Frederick Law, 13, 29, 92, 152
Orchard Beach Park. *See* Moses, Robert, N.Y.C. parks
Orient Point State Park. *See* Moses, Robert, N.Y. State parks
Papp, Joseph, Shakespeare in the Park, 39
Patterson, A. Holly, 138, 183
Pope, John Russell, 156
Powell, Rev. Adam Clayton, Jr., 42
Power Broker, The (Caro), 14, 22, 23, 24, 29, 31, 32, 35–42, 44, 47–53, 69, 103, 199
Prospect Expressway. *See* Moses, Robert, parkways
Public Works Administration (PWA), 72, 73, 74, 76, 192, 196
Queens-Midtown Tunnel, 102, 103
Rabenold, Elwood M., 50
Reconstruction Finance Corporation (RFC), 71, 72, 73, 74, 75, 76
Regional Plan Association, 29
Ribicoff, Abraham, 85
Riverside Park. *See* Moses, Robert, public works
"Robert Moses, Bridgebuilder," (Marilyn Weigold), 16
Robert Taylor Homes, Chicago, compared to Moses' public housing, 25

Rockaway Improvement. *See* Moses, Robert, public works
Rockefeller, Nelson, 21, 48, 79, 82–86, 87, 114
Ronan, William J., 84
Roosevelt, Franklin Delano, 21, 70, 72, 73, 74, 101, 102
Shadgen, Joseph, promoter of 1939 World's Fair, 93, 112
Shea Stadium. *See* Moses, Robert, public works
Smith, Alfred E., 21, 40, 59
South Bronx. *See* Moses, Robert, public housing
Southern State Parkway. *See* Moses, Robert, parkways
Sprague, J. Russel, 182, 183
Starr, Roger, 17
Streetcar Suburbs (Warner, Jr.), 43
Sunken Meadow State Park. *See* Moses, Robert, N.Y. State parks
Throgs Neck Bridge. *See* Moses, Robert, bridges
Tobin, Austin, 60, 61, 62, 63, 64
Triborough Bridge. *See* Moses, Robert, bridges
Tselos, George, paper describing Moses' official and personal correspondence, 16
United Nations building. *See* Moses, Robert, public works
Valley Stream State Park. *See* Moses, Robert, N.Y. State parks
Vanderbilt, William Kissam, Jr., 151–53, 155–58
Van Wyck Expressway. *See* Moses, Robert, parkways
Verrazano Narrows Bridge. *See* Moses, Robert, bridges
Vinoly, Raphael, 216
Wagner, Robert F., 21
Walker, James J., 103
Wantagh State Parkway. *See* Moses, Robert, parkways
Warner, Sam Bass, Jr., 43
West Side Highway. *See* Moses, Robert, parkways
Whitestone Expressway. *See* Moses, Robert, parkways
Woodward, C. Vann, 42
World's Fair, 1939. *See* Moses, Robert, public works
World's Fair, 1964. *See* Moses, Robert, public works

Also available:

Long Island Studies
Evoking a Sense of Place
edited by Joann P. Krieg
196 pages, illustrations, indexed
ISBN: 1-55787-022-5 — 1988 — $14.00

> *If, as John Dewey claimed, locality is truly the only reality, then to evoke a "sense of place," we must know the history and culture of a community. Only thus can we understand ourselves in time and space. The essays in this volume contribute to understanding varied aspects of Long Island's rich heritage.*
> "Introduction," by Natalie A. Naylor, Director,
> Long Island Studies Institute

At Hofstra University in May 1986, over 400 people met to discuss and learn more about the history and culture of Long Island. This volume contains papers presented at the conference.

They focus on topics in material culture ranging from archaeological evidence of Native Americans to colonial household inventories in Suffolk County, and the Dutch Colonial Revival homes. Papers on commerce and transportation include colonial Oyster Bay's international trade, the early years of the Long Island Railroad, pioneer women aviators, and the Ocean Parkway. Cultural and social history papers are devoted to Long Island Quakers, Jupiter Hammon, the Samuel Jones murder case, North Beach Resort, and Italian Americans. An extensive bibliography and resource section has been added for researchers.

Typeset on an Itek Digitek 3000 photocompositor in 11½ point Palatino® Medium on a 12½ baseline with heads in Italic and Semibold Italic.

Printed on 60 pound white and perfect bound in 10 point coated-one-side cover.

Contact Walt Steesy for your book publishing needs.

A *quality* publication from
Heart of the Lakes Publishing
Interlaken, New York 14847